Symbols and Reality

Reading the Bible as Literature

How Bible Stories Work: A Guided Study of Biblical Narrative

Sweeter Than Honey, Richer Than Gold: A Guided Study of Biblical Poetry

Letters of Grace & Beauty: A Guided Literary Study of New Testament Epistles

Jesus the Hero: A Guided Literary Study of the Gospels

Symbols and Reality: A Guided Study of Prophecy, Apocalypse, and Visionary Literature

Short Sentences Long Remembered: A Guided Study of Proverbs and Other Wisdom Literature

READING
THE BIBLE AS
LITERATURE

Symbols and Reality

A GUIDED STUDY OF
PROPHECY, APOCALYPSE,
AND VISIONARY LITERATURE

LELAND RYKEN

WEAVER BOOK
COMPANY

Symbols and Reality: A Guided Study of Prophecy, Apocalypse, and Visionary Literature
© 2016 by Leland Ryken

Published by
Weaver Book Company
1190 Summerset Dr.
Wooster, OH 44691
weaverbookcompany.com

Cover design and interior layout: Frank Gutbrod

Library of Congress Cataloging-in-Publication Data
Ryken, Leland, author.

Symbols and reality : a guided study of prophecy, apocalypse,
and visionary literature / Leland Ryken.
Wooster : Weaver Book Company, 2016. | Series: Reading the Bible as literature

LCCN 2016020699 | ISBN 9781941337608

LCSH: Apocalyptic literature--History and criticism. | Bible--Prophecies.
LCC BS646 .R95 2016
DDC 220/.046--dc23 LC record available at https://lccn.loc.gov/

2016020699

Printed in the United States of America
16 17 18 19 20 / 5 4 3 2 1

Contents

Series Preface

This series is part of the mission of Weaver Book Company to equip Christians to understand and teach the Bible effectively by giving them reliable tools for handling the biblical text. Within that landscape, the niche that my volumes are designed to fill is the literary approach to the Bible. This has been my scholarly passion for nearly half a century. It is my belief that a literary approach to the Bible is the common reader's friend, in contrast to more specialized types of scholarship on the Bible.

Nonetheless, the literary approach to the Bible needs to be defended against legitimate fears by evangelical Christians, and through the years I have not scorned to clear the territory of misconceptions as part of my defense of a literary analysis of the Bible. In kernel form, my message has been this:

1. To view the Bible as literature is not a suspect modern idea, nor does it need to imply theological liberalism. The idea of the Bible as literature began with the writers of the Bible, who display literary qualities in their writings and who refer with technical precision to a wide range of literary genres such as psalm, proverb, parable, apocalypse, and many more.

2. Although fiction is a common trait of literature, it is not an essential feature of it. A work of literature can be replete with literary technique and artifice while remaining historically factual.

3. To approach the Bible as literature need not be characterized by viewing the Bible *only* as literature, any more than reading it as history requires us to see only the history of the Bible.

4. When we see literary qualities in the Bible we are not attempting to bring the Bible down to the level of ordinary literature; it is simply an objective statement about the inherent nature of the Bible. The Bible can be trusted to reveal its extraordinary qualities if we approach it with ordinary methods of literary analysis.

To sum up, it would be tragic if we allowed ourselves to be deprived of literary methods of analyzing the Bible by claims that are fallacies.

What, then, does it mean to approach the Bible as literature? A literary study of the Bible should begin where any other approach begins—by accepting as true all that the biblical writers claim about their book. These claims include its inspiration and super-intendence by God, its infallibility, its historical truthfulness, its unique power to infiltrate people's lives, and its supreme authority.

With that as a foundation, a literary approach to the Bible is characterized by the following traits:

1. A literary approach acknowledges that the Bible comes to us in a predominantly literary format. In the words of C. S. Lewis, "There is a . . . sense in which the Bible, since it is after all literature, cannot properly be read except as literature; and the different parts of it as the different sorts

of literature they are."[1] The overall format of the Bible is that of an anthology of literature.

2. In keeping with that, a literary approach identifies the genres and other literary forms of the Bible and analyzes individual texts in keeping with those forms. An awareness of literary genres and forms programs how we analyze a biblical text and opens doors into a text that would otherwise remain closed.

3. A literary approach begins with the premise that a work of literature embodies universal human experience. Such truthfulness to human experience is complementary to the tendency of traditional approaches to the Bible to mainly see ideas in it. A literary approach corrects a commonly held fallacy that the Bible is a theology book with proof texts attached.

4. A literary approach to the Bible is ready to grant value to the biblical authors' skill with language and literary technique, seeing these as an added avenue to our enjoyment of the Bible.

5. A literary approach to the Bible takes its humble place alongside the two other main approaches—the theological and the historical. These three domains are established by the biblical writers themselves, who usually combine all three elements in their writings. However, in terms of space, the Bible is a predominantly literary book. Usually the historical and theological material is packaged in literary form.

These traits and methods of literary analysis govern the content of my series of guided studies to the genres of the Bible.

Although individual books in my series are organized by the leading literary genres that appear in the Bible, I need to highlight

---

1   *Reflections on the Psalms* (New York: Harcourt, Brace & World, 1958), 3.

that all of these genres have certain traits in common. Literature itself, en masse, makes up a homogenous whole. In fact, we can speak of *literature as a genre* (the title of the opening chapter of a book titled *Kinds of Literature*).[2] The traits that make up literature as a genre will simply be assumed in the volumes in this series. They include the following: universal, recognizable human experience concretely embodied as the subject matter; the packaging of this subject matter in distinctly literary genres; the authors' use of special resources of language that set their writing apart from everyday expository discourse; and stylistic excellence and other forms of artistry that are part of the beauty of a work of literature.

What are the advantages that come from applying the methods of literary analysis? In brief, they are as follows: an improved method of interacting with biblical texts in terms of the type of writing that they are; doing justice to the specificity of texts (again because the approach is tailored to the genres of a text); ability to see unifying patterns in a text; relating texts to everyday human experience; and enjoyment of the artistic skill of biblical authors.

Summary

A book needs to be read in keeping with its author's intention. We can see from the Bible itself that it is a thoroughly literary book. God superintended its authors to write a very (though not wholly) literary book. To pay adequate attention to the literary qualities of the Bible not only helps to unlock the meanings of the Bible; it is also a way of honoring the literary intentions of its authors. Surely biblical authors regarded everything that they put into their writing as important. We also need to regard those things as important.

---

2   Alastair Fowler, *Kinds of Literature: An Introduction to the Theory of Genres and Modes* (Oxford: Oxford University Press, 1985).

Introduction

F or multiple reasons, the parts of the Bible covered in this guide are the most difficult ones to read and understand. The first step in mastering the prophetic and apocalyptic parts of the Bible is to acknowledge the difficulties posed by them. Once we understand the nature of the difficulties, we are in a position to find solutions. This introduction covers three topics: facing the fact that these biblical genres are difficult; analyzing what makes these forms difficult; and learning how we can feel confident in mastering these parts of the Bible.

Admitting That We Feel Intimidated

Before we can determine why the prophetic and apocalyptic parts of the Bible are intimidating to us, we need to have the forthrightness to acknowledge that they *are* problematical. No statistical data exists to prove this, so I simply pose the following questions:

- In the past two years, have you chosen Jeremiah, Ezekiel, or Revelation for your daily devotional reading?
- When you choose a prophetic or apocalyptic book for daily devotions, do you stick with it to the end?

- Have you heard a sermon series based on these parts of the Bible in the past two years?
- If you were asked to teach a six-week session to a Sunday school class, would you choose to teach part of Jeremiah or Zechariah?

I am going to hazard the guess that the number of people who answered yes to those questions is so few as to be statistically insignificant. By contrast, I think it likely that other parts of the Bible are regularly used in the ways I have named in my questions.

No one should feel guilty about finding the prophetic and apocalyptic parts of the Bible difficult. They are as they are. Nor is anything positive gained by denying that we lack confidence in dealing with these books in the Bible. Acknowledging our perplexity about the prophetic, apocalyptic, and visionary parts of the Bible is the starting point for making them an open book instead of a closed book.

Obstacles

All we need to do to identify the difficulty that we face with prophetic and apocalyptic parts of the Bible is to browse them for half an hour. If we dip into a representative range (not limiting ourselves to just one biblical book), we find the following difficulties.

Abundance of Obscure Geographic Place Names

The Old Testament prophetic books are filled with references to nations and cities of the ancient world that are unfamiliar to us. Even if we look up the information about them in a study Bible or commentary, the names remain mere names and nothing specific. Here is an example:

> Therefore I wail for Moab;
>   I cry out for all Moab,
>   for the men of Kir-hareseth I mourn.
> More than for Jazer I weep for you,
>   O vine of Sibmah! (Jer. 48:31–32)

Many of the Old Testament prophecies are directed to nations and groups such as those in the quoted passage. It is simply part of prophetic discourse. The problem is that modern readers find the references unintelligible or mere abstractions.

Obscurity

The enigmatic place names are a specific manifestation of a more general obscurity that frequently confronts us in the prophetic and apocalyptic parts of the Bible. Creating disorientation seems to have been part of the strategy of the prophets and writers of apocalypse, perhaps as a way of shaking people out of their complacency and inattentiveness. Here is an example:

> The oracle concerning Dumah.
> One is calling to me from Seir,
>   "Watchman, what time of the night?
>   Watchman, what time of the night?"
> The watchman says:
> "Morning comes, and also the night.
>   If you will inquire, inquire;
>   come back again." (Isa. 21:11–12)

The obvious question is, What does this mean? It is no wonder that we often find ourselves bewildered and therefore intimidated by prophetic discourse.

Topicality

Much prophetic discourse is rooted in specific conditions. Literary scholars speak of "topicality" in regard to this, meaning that the passage under consideration makes references to topics or situations that existed in the prophet's time and would have been understood by people living then but not by people living now. The term "topicality" implies that such references to contemporary events pose a problem for modern readers, and in fact literary scholars often speak of *excessive* topicality as characterizing certain genres such as satire. An informal rule of thumb is that if a detail in a passage requires a footnote to explain it for modern readers, the passage falls under the rubric of being topical. Here is an example:

> Ah, land of whirring wings
>   that is beyond the rivers of Cush,
> which sends ambassadors by the sea,
>   in vessels of papyrus on the waters! (Isa. 18:1–2)

Some nation has been doing something noteworthy. Probably people living at the time knew who and what made up the story, but for us it is a head-scratcher.

Poetry and Symbolism

Not all poetry and symbolism is difficult and obscure, but much of it in prophetic and apocalyptic discourse *is* elusive and difficult. Consider this example:

> "Behold, the days are coming," declares the LORD,
>   "when the plowman shall overtake the reaper
>   and the treader of grapes him who sows the seed;
> the mountains shall drip sweet wine,
>   and all the hills shall flow with it." (Amos 9:13)

It is obvious that these things cannot happen literally, so what do they mean figuratively? What does it mean that the plowman will overtake the reaper? How can mountains drip with wine, and what reality does the figurative statement delineate?

Code Language

The claim that vast parts of the Bible are a code language that needs to be cracked is something that I resist. But there is one genre where I think the concept is valid, namely, apocalyptic writing. It seems likely that some of the details in the book of Revelation that baffle us had an understood meaning at the time. The book of Revelation may even have been what we know as *underground literature* that criticized the tyrannical and anti-Christian Roman Empire in a concealed way. The extended lament over the fall of Babylon in Revelation 18 is an example. This communal entity, personified as a woman, is portrayed as a worldwide empire and mercantile success. The nation of Babylon had been off the historical stage for centuries, so it seems plausible that "Babylon" is John's code language for "Rome."

Repetitiousness

The two dominant modes in prophecy are the oracle of judgment and the oracle of redemption. The recurrent unit in apocalyptic literature is the vision of either calamity and woe or redemption and heavenly bliss. In the prophetic and apocalyptic books we get huge blocks of one or another of these, as anyone who has read these books through one chapter per day can testify. A given day's reading seems like "more of the same," and a law of diminishing return sets in.

Uncertainty about the Referent

The word "referent" in this context means the reality that is being referred to. Some of the categories I have discussed above are bifocal, by which I mean that the surface of the biblical text stands for or is a picture of something else. Double meaning is a basic method of operation in prophetic and apocalyptic discourse. For example, in the portrait of Christ in Revelation 1:12–16, such details as a long robe and white hair and a sharp sword coming out of his mouth obviously *stand for* something else. In Amos, the prediction that the mountains will drip with wine *symbolizes* something other than a literal picture. As we assimilate such passages, we naturally search for the referent—the thing *to which* the surface details point. Left to our own devices, we often struggle, and even the experts often do not agree on their interpretations. It is no wonder that prophetic and apocalyptic books intimidate us as we face the need to identify the referent of the surface details.

The Problem of Prophetic and Apocalyptic Time

As an extension of the problem of finding the referent, it is often a toss-up as we seek to determine the time that is in view in a prophetic or apocalyptic passage. Here is an example:

> On that day there shall be a fountain opened for the house of David and the inhabitants of Jerusalem, to cleanse them from sin and uncleanness. (Zech. 13:1)

Is this a picture of the imminent future, namely, the return of a remnant from Babylonian captivity to resettle Jerusalem? Is the prophet Zechariah looking forward six hundred years to the incarnation of Jesus and the blessings that this brought permanently into the world? Is this an apocalyptic vision of the New Jerusalem of the millennium and eternity? Might all of these be simultaneously in view?

Wondering What the Relevance Is

Many of the events described and predicted in the Old Testament prophetic books happened centuries and millennia ago. For example, Isaiah 14 consists of oracles predicting the destruction of Babylon, Assyria, and Philistia. The prophecies were fulfilled soon after Isaiah declared them. What relevance and edification are there for us in these chapters from ancient history? The second half of the book of Daniel contains visions of a succession of world empires that came and went. How does that help us with daily living?

Taking Stock of the Difficulties

The foregoing discussion of difficulties posed by prophetic and apocalyptic writing serves several functions. First, the traits I have listed as difficulties are at the same time an introduction to leading features of prophetic and apocalyptic literature. I have made a substantial start to providing an account of the literary forms covered in this guide.

Second, to name something is partly to master it. If counselors can get clients to talk about their fears and anxieties, that very naming of the foe is the first step to conquering it. Something similar is true in regard to the difficulties that we feel in regard to prophetic and apocalyptic literature.

Third, we can undertake our journey toward mastering these biblical forms with confidence that God wants us to enjoy and understand the prophetic and apocalyptic books in the Bible. The very fact that this material appears in the Bible proves that. We have all the incentive we need for tackling the prophecies and visions of the Bible with zest and expectation. If they matter to God (as evidenced by their being in the Bible), they need to matter to us. The very fact that these forms occupy such a major share of the Bible adds to our incentive. These are major biblical genres and therefore important to us.

Fourth, I would not have written this guide if I were not confident that solutions exist to the problems posed by prophetic and apocalyptic literature. Every literary form has its identifiable traits and accompanying rules for interpretation. All we need is a guide through the territory.

Defining Prophecy, Apocalypse, and Visionary Literature

The purpose of this chapter is to provide a preliminary overview of the three major literary forms covered in this book—prophecy, apocalypse, and visionary literature. My aim is to give the proverbial "lay of the land," treating the three forms more as categories or branches of literature than genres, though it is not inaccurate to call them "genres." Later chapters in this book scrutinize the specific genres that make up these parts of the Bible. This chapter is like an orientation meeting for a tour group in which the leader describes general features and traits of a country of destination, without getting into any of the specific places that the tour will visit within that country.

Prophecy

We need to begin with a statement of what prophecy is not: the primary trait of prophecy in the Bible is not that it foretells the future. Much less of the prophetic books is futuristic than is commonly thought. In saying that, I particularly have the distant and eschatological (end-times) future in view. It is true that prophets often predict imminent judgment or deliverance for people and nations, but we assimilate these soon-to-happen events much as we assimilate a prediction that someone who habitually exceeds the speed limit "will certainly get arrested." We think of it as a comment on the status quo rather than the future. We can say without reservation that a biblical prophet is someone whose primary task is to speak or "tell forth" messages from God rather than foretell the future—*forthtelling* rather than *foretelling*.

Prophetic literature starts with a religious group in ancient Judaism known as prophets. Prophets were very prominent figures in Hebrew society. Their high stature is perhaps best seen in the easy access they had to the ruling king in his court. Even evil kings often took the initiative in inviting hostile prophets into their court to hear what they had to say. To catch the flavor of how prophets could trump even priests and monarchs, we need only picture the prophet Nathan standing in David's inner chamber and proclaiming, "You are the man!" (2 Sam. 12:7).

Prophets fulfilled the task of speaking from God to his people (in contrast to priests, who represented people to God). The prophetic books of the Bible can be defined as the books that contain the messages of a prophet, which in their original form were uttered orally and later written down. To define a prophecy by its point of origin (a prophet) and its status as a message from God to people says nothing about the literary forms that appear in a prophetic book. Those forms occupy later chapters in this guide. The label of "prophecy" signals a broad category that by itself is less descriptive of a prophetic book than scholars often imply.

If the term "prophecy" thus mainly signals the content of a prophetic book rather than its literary forms, what characterizes the content of a prophetic book? The first answer is that prophets were primarily concerned with the moral and spiritual life of individuals and the nation or believing community in the here and now. The Old Testament prophets were keen observers of their own time. Today we would speak of social and moral critique as the overall category of much (not all) prophetic writing. As the prophets looked at the contemporary national and international scene, they were primarily critical of it. Delineation of evil accompanied by denunciation of it and prediction of divine judgment against it account for the bulk of prophetic writing. The dominant harshness of prophetic discourse is balanced by consolation and the promise of God's favor. The latter gets somewhat less space, but together the twin themes of judgment and consolation make up the prophetic books of the Bible.

LEARNING BY DOING

The following passage (excerpts from Ezekiel 34) is a typical example of prophetic literature. You can test your mastery of the preceding description of prophecy by applying the generalizations to this passage.

> The word of the LORD came to me: "Son of man, prophesy against the shepherds of Israel; prophesy, and say to them, even to the shepherds, Thus says the Lord GOD: Ah, shepherds of Israel who have been feeding yourselves! Should not shepherds feed the sheep? You eat the fat, you clothe yourselves with the wool, you slaughter the fat ones, but you do not feed the sheep. The weak you have not strengthened, the sick you have not healed, the injured you have not bound up, the strayed you have not brought back, the lost you have not sought, and with

force and harshness you have ruled them. So they were scattered, because there was no shepherd, and they became food for all the wild beasts . . .

"For thus says the Lord GOD: Behold, I, I myself will search for my sheep and will seek them out. As a shepherd seeks out his flock when he is among his sheep that have been scattered, so will I seek out my sheep, and I will rescue them from all places where they have been scattered on a day of clouds and thick darkness . . . I will feed them with good pasture, and on the mountain heights of Israel shall be their grazing land. There they shall lie down in good grazing land, and on rich pasture they shall feed on the mountains of Israel."

Apocalypse

Apocalyptic writing at first glance seems similar to prophecy, but the differences between the two are more extensive than the similarities. What is similar is the authoritative voice of the writer or speaker. Prophecy and apocalypse are both a revelation from God. They strike us as coming from a world beyond and as disclosing a type of truth that human imagination by itself would not produce. Additionally, there is overlap of the general content of the two types of discourse. Both denounce evil as it exists in the world, and both predict God's punishment of it now and in the future.

But if we look more closely, the two genres begin to reveal their differences. For example, the prophet's portrayal of contemporary evil tends to be direct and specific, yielding a picture of what is happening in a specific society of the prophet's time. The portrayal of evil in apocalyptic writing tends to be more generalized and symbolic. A prophet denounces contemporary evil this way:

> The daughters of Zion are haughty
>> and walk with outstretched necks,
>> glancing wantonly with their eyes,
> mincing along as they go,
>> tinkling with their feet. (Isa. 3:16)

Apocalyptic portrayal of evil is a universalized picture of cosmic evil, as in the following passage:

> And I saw a beast rising out of the sea, with ten horns and seven heads, with ten diadems on its horns and blasphemous names on its heads. (Rev. 13:1)

More important than the differing ways of portraying life on earth is the futuristic orientation of apocalyptic writing. We can loosely identify apocalyptic writing as end-times discourse, also called "visions of the end." A qualification that immediately needs to be made is that the end-times in Christian apocalypse extend for a very long time. In fact, there is a strand in the New Testament that views the entire time after the incarnation of Jesus as "the last days" (or "the latter days"). The following is a typical apocalyptic passage portraying what will happen in the future:

> When he [the Lamb] opened the second seal, I heard the second living creature say, "Come!" And out came another horse, bright red. Its rider was permitted to take peace from the earth, so that people should slay one another, and he was given a great sword. (Rev. 6:3–4)

One of the things that make prophecy and apocalypse difficult to keep separate is that there are apocalyptic visions in the Old Testament prophetic books. In fact, a prophetic book like Zechariah is primarily an apocalyptic vision. On the other hand, there is an informal test of whether a passage is prophetic or apocalyptic. The primary form of prophecy is the oracle—a message from God, frequently bearing either the formula or sense of "thus says the LORD." The prophet is preeminently a person who has *heard* a message from God. The primary form of apocalypse is the vision, most frequently accompanied by the formula of what the author has *seen* or what God has *shown*. Because apocalyptic discourse is about the end, a certain tone of finality permeates it.

LEARNING BY DOING

The following apocalyptic passage will enable you to apply the description that was given above:

> At that time shall arise Michael, the great prince who has charge of your people. And there shall be a time of trouble, such as never has been since there was a nation till that time. But at that time your people shall be delivered, everyone whose name shall be found written in the book. And many of those who sleep in the dust of the earth shall awake, some to everlasting life, and some to shame and everlasting contempt. And those who are wise shall shine like the brightness of the sky above; and those who turn many to righteousness, like the stars forever and ever. (Dan. 12:1–3)

Visionary Literature

Visionary writing is a broad and amorphous category, as are prophecy and apocalypse. To get a grip on it, we need to take a wide-angle view of literature as a whole. Literature exists on a continuum in regard to the degree of realism or fantasy in it. At one end of the literary continuum is realism. It may be fictional or nonfictional, but in both cases it does not violate the rules of reality. There are no flying houses or red horses in the real world. Realism is based on the principle of *verisimilitude*, meaning lifelikeness.

At the other end of the literary continuum is fantasy. Fantasy is not composed *entirely* of unlifelike details, but to varying degrees it departs from what we find in the world around us. A story in which animals talk like humans and perform human actions is a fantasy story. The Narnia stories of C. S. Lewis combine everyday reality with fantasy, but since the fantasy elements are foregrounded, we have no hesitation in classifying the books as fantasy. The adjective "visionary" is synonymous with literary fantasy. It includes a heavy incidence of unlifelikeness. The following portrayal of an invasion of locusts is the product of the fantastic imagination rather than the realistic imagination:

> Their appearance is like the appearance of horses
>> and like war horses they run.
> As with the rumbling of chariots,
>> they leap on the tops of the mountains,
> like the crackling of a flame of fire
>> devouring the stubble,
> like a powerful army
>> drawn up for battle.
> Before them peoples are in anguish;
>> all faces grow pale. (Joel 2:4–6)

In visionary writing in the Bible, the unlifelike details *portray* real people and events. The visionary element is the unrealistic or unlifelike vehicle by which reality is delineated.

For those who might be unsettled by the thought of fantasy in the Bible, we can note that figures of speech such as metaphor, hyperbole, and symbol are a form of unlifelikeness or fantasy. God is not really a rock (Ps. 18:31). The warrior David did not actually beat his enemies fine as dust (Ps. 18:42). Those who believe in God are not literally able to "tread on the lion" (Ps. 91:13). These are elements of fantasy that portray reality and truth.

Whereas prophecy and apocalypse are broad categories of literature defined partly by their characteristic content, visionary writing is what literary scholars call a "mode" that can appear in many different genres and categories of writing. The relevance of that to this guide is that both prophecy and apocalypse contain a heavy incidence of visionary writing. This visionary element is a quality that brings prophecy and apocalypse together. In turn, this overlapping of categories and forms makes the biblical material covered in this guide difficult to master.

Simply knowing that visionary writing depends on the fantastic and unlifelike as its basic mode does not yield a method of analyzing a passage, but it alerts us to the nature of the passage and enables us to pick up on qualities that might otherwise remain vague and unnoticed. Additionally, the fantastic or visionary imagination is entertaining. But visionary writing is more than entertaining: by means of the fantastic imagination, we are led to see reality more precisely than we otherwise would. To take the example of the super-locusts quoted above, our first response might be, How ever did you think of that? But then it dawns on us that we experience the terror of a locust invasion all the more vividly because of the element of fantasy.

LEARNING BY DOING

One of my favorite pieces of visionary writing is one that involves a woman named Wickedness sitting inside a cereal container. It appears below and will enable you to apply what the preceding discussion has taught:

Then the angel who talked with me came forward and said to me, "Lift your eyes and see what this is that is going out." And I said, "What is it?" He said, "This is the basket that is going out." And he said, "This is their iniquity in all the land." And behold, the leaden cover was lifted, and there was a woman sitting in the basket! And he said, "This is Wickedness." And he thrust her back into the basket, and thrust down the leaden weight on its opening.

Then I lifted my eyes and saw, and behold, two women coming forward! The wind was in their wings. They had wings like the wings of a stork, and they lifted up the basket between earth and heaven. Then I said to the angel who talked with me, "Where are they taking the basket?" He said to me, "To the land of Shinar, to build a house for it. And when this is prepared, they will set the basket down there on its base." (Zech. 5:5–11)

Time in Prophecy and Apocalypse

An additional complicating element in prophecy and apocalypse is the way in which time is presented. Some of the references, especially in prophecy, are contemporaneous with the author and are referred to in the present tense.

Stretching outward from the present is an expansive future. We can plot this future on a timeline with three main stages. These stages can also be viewed as categories of prophetic events, as the following outline shows:

- *The immediate or near future.* The point of reference for this category is the time at which the prophet spoke or wrote. An example of the immediate future is the following: "Within a year . . . all the glory of Kedar will come to an end" (Isa. 21:16). Even if the predicted event is fifty years later, it still falls into the category of "near future" or "imminent." An example is the oracle against Jerusalem pronounced in Isaiah 22, which predicts events that happened shortly after Isaiah lived. Even though the events that encompassed the end of the kingdoms of Israel and Judah and the return to Israel after the Babylonian captivity covered a considerable span of time, it is useful to combine all of those events together under the heading of "the immediate and near future." The rationale is that references to the destruction of Israel and Judah and the Babylonian captivity belong to an ancient era that ended before the other stages on the timeline occurred, and we need a way to seal them off in ancient history.

- *The intermediate future.* The intermediate future on the prophetic timeline is the incarnation and earthly life of Jesus, the Messiah. The messianic prophecies of the Old Testament prophets belong to the midpoint on the prophetic continuum. The fulfillment came centuries after the lives of the Old Testament prophets, but also millennia before the end of human history. The messianic prophecies are thus a category of their own.

- *The eschatological (end-times) future*, also called "the apocalyptic future." These prophecies predict what will happen as history winds its way to its final end. The qualification that needs to be made is that "the latter days" cover a very long time in prophetic discourse. Some of the predictions made by Jesus in his apocalyptic discourses and John in the book of Revelation were future for people living then (such as the fall of Jerusalem in AD 70) but past for us. Other events in those same discourses occur perpetually as fallen history keeps getting worse. For example, the visions in Revelation of moral degeneration and the collapse of nature were future for John but are daily reality for us.

The foregoing timeline is generally easy to apply. A complexity sometimes arises as to whether a given passage refers to certain realities that entered human history with the incarnation of Jesus and the salvation that this achieved, or whether the passage portrays realities that will not occur until the end of history. The more poetic, symbolic, or visionary a passage is, the more open-ended it is, capable of being viewed as referring to both the blessings of the messianic age and the eschaton at the end of history.

The following passage provides a good test case:

I will rejoice in Jerusalem
    and be glad in my people;
no more shall be heard in it the sound of weeping
    and the cry of distress.
No more shall there be in it
    an infant who lives but a few days,
    or an old man who does not fill out his days,
for the young man shall die a hundred years old,
    and the sinner a hundred years old shall be accursed.
(Isa. 65:19–20)

Is this a symbolic account of the return of a remnant to Jerusalem after the Babylonian captivity, or the blessings of the messianic age that started with the incarnation of Jesus, or the final millennium and eternal life in heaven? It is entirely defensible to regard all of these as being the referent of the description.

Prophetic Oracles

Many parts of the Bible are a loosely organized collection of numerous individual genres and literary forms. Scholars therefore use such labels as the following to identify this mixture: "hybrid form," "mixed-genre format," "encyclopedic form," "anthology," or" miscellany." Simply knowing that parts of the Bible fall into these categories helps us to impose a unity on the material. The very mixture of forms imparts unity.

This chapter explores the three main forms that make up the prophetic books—depiction of evil, denunciation of evil, and coming punishment of evil. That leaves further genres to explore in the two following chapters, so this chapter should be assimilated as an initial foray into the territory and not as the last word on the prophetic books.

Oracle

An oracle is a pronouncement or message from God to people. Often this message is imparted through an intermediary agent, namely, a prophet. The prophetic books of the Bible consist mainly of oracles from God. Our sense that everything is coming from God is kept alive by certain formulas. For example, the statement "thus says the LORD" appears nearly four hundred times in the Old Testament prophetic books. There are approximately two hundred references to "the word of the LORD."

It is true that sometimes the messenger formula is absent, and that a passage is expressed by the prophet in his own voice. However, because such proclamations from the prophet appear in a prophetic book, we assimilate them exactly as we do the messages that are ascribed to God, namely, as an authoritative message from God.

An oracle is usually expressed in formal language and is elevated in style above the chatter at the bus stop. For example, many prophetic oracles are expressed as poetry, including both poetic language and the verse form of parallelism. The adjectival form of the word "oracle, "oracular," hints at this formality, with the word implying a tone of authority. An oracle comes as something that needs to be heeded, not an email from a colleague.

There are three main categories of oracle in the prophetic books. This does not mean that every oracle falls decisively into these categories, but they constitute the main contours of what we find as we read the prophetic books. Even though there are three main types, an even more foundational principle of organization is a dichotomy between bad-news oracles and good-news oracles.

Oracle of Judgment

An oracle of judgment is a pronouncement of judgment against evil. The ultimate origin of that judgment is God, and the judgment is a punishment for disobedience. An oracle can be voiced as coming directly from God, or it can be expressed by the prophet as a message that he received from God to pass on to a corrupt group or society. An example of the former is the following (Jer. 6:19), which is not said to be a word from God to the prophet but is presented directly:

Hear, O earth; behold, I am bringing disaster upon this people,
> the fruit of their devices,
because they have not paid attention to my words;
> and as for my law, they have rejected it.

By contrast, the oracle found in Jeremiah 14:1–12 begins with the lead-in, "The word of the LORD that came to Jeremiah concerning the drought." Or a prophet might simply denounce evil in his own voice: "Woe to those who are wise in their own eyes" (Isa. 5:21).

The foundational premise of an oracle of judgment is that it takes human failing and evil as its subject. With that as a "given," prophets do as many as three things:

- portray evil
- denounce the evil that has been portrayed
- predict coming judgment or punishment of the evil

These categories provide a very helpful analytic framework for understanding and teaching an oracle of judgment. We should note, however, that a given oracle of judgment might not include all three ingredients, with the result that we should not try to force every oracle of judgment into the composite format.

Each of the three categories can be subjected to analysis. As we ponder the *portrayal of evil*, we can look for the following traits and distinctions:

- The form in which the portrayal of evil is embodied is either a catalog or list of vices, or a portrait of wrongdoers.
- Some of the evil portrayed is moral evil (directed against fellow humans), and some of it is spiritual evil (directed against God).

- Sometimes individuals are portrayed as the evildoer, sometimes a group within society, and sometimes an entire society
  or nation.
- Sometimes the evil is portrayed by means of generalized
  abstractions, and at other times we get very specific
  pictures of wrongdoing.

In regard to the prophet's *denunciation of evil*, we can also
discern certain distinctions, as follows:

- Sometimes God accuses an individual or a group, and we
  assimilate this indictment as God's denunciation of evil and
  those who commit it. An example is Malachi 2:8, where God
  accuses the priests: "You have turned aside from the way. You
  have caused many to stumble by your instruction. You have
  corrupted the covenant of Levi, says the LORD of hosts."
- At other times the prophet denounces a practice or a
  group. For example, the woe formula is common in
  prophetic discourse: "Woe to those who are at ease in
  Zion" (Amos 6:1). Or this: "Hear this word, you cows
  [wealthy women] of Jerusalem" (Amos 4:1). This is not an
  accusation but a denunciation.
- Much of the time the prophet simply assumes that the
  reader's moral and spiritual outlook is correct, so that
  the mere portrayal of evil will be understood to be a
  denunciation of it.

The third item on the framework, the *prediction of judgment
against evildoers*, can also be put to analytic use, as follows:

- There is actually quite a range of judgments that enter the
  composite oracles of judgment. Sometimes God promises
  to destroy evil and evildoers. Sometimes he predicts
  that a foreign nation will conquer a godless or immoral

society. Sometimes God says that he will turn a deaf ear to evildoers who clamor for relief, in effect turning the evildoers over to their own self-destructive tendencies (see Jer. 11:11–13 for an example). Often the prophet simply paints graphic pictures of coming desolation, which we assimilate as a prediction of judgment.

- There is also a range in regard to the timetable for coming judgment. Sometimes the time for judgment is not spelled out. At other times we are given to understand that foreign nations are gradually preparing an invasion. Sometimes we learn that the time for reform is past and that the collapse of the nation is imminent. At other times we get the impression that the judgment in view is final, apocalyptic judgment at the end of time.

To summarize, the basic paradigm of the oracle of judgment is a threefold pattern—depiction of evil, denunciation of evil, and coming punishment of evil. As we look at these three, we can discern additional angles. The depiction of evil is the understood reason for the judgment or punishment that is predicted. The prediction of coming punishment casts a tone of warning over the portrayal and denunciation of evil.

LEARNING BY DOING

The following oracle of judgment will enable you to put the fore-going theory into practice.

> Shall I acquit the man with wicked scales
> and with a bag of deceitful weights?
> Your rich men are full of violence;
> your inhabitants speak lies,

> and their tongue is deceitful in their mouth.
> Therefore I strike you with a grievous blow,
> making you desolate because of your sins.
> You shall eat, but not be satisfied,
> and there shall be hunger within you;
> you shall put away, but not preserve,
> and what you preserve I will give to the sword.
> You shall sow, but not reap;
> you shall tread olives, but not anoint yourselves with oil;
> you shall tread grapes, but not drink wine. (Micah 6:11–15)

Oracle of Blessing

An oracle of blessing pronounces or predicts blessing on a group or nation. As with the oracle of judgment, the pronouncement is sometimes phrased as coming directly from God, and other times as a message that God entrusted the prophet to deliver. To anticipate the following section of this chapter, an oracle of blessing simply announces blessings, whereas an oracle of redemption or salvation implies a return to favor with God after a time of rejection or suffering. Sometimes the oracle of blessing and the oracle of redemption overlap or merge, and we need not agonize to find differences where they do not exist. For example, the pronouncement of blessings can be phrased as a promise for the future instead of a description of the present, but without a strong sense of restitution of what has been lost through God's judgment against human waywardness (a feature of the oracle of salvation).

The staple of an oracle of blessing is the list or catalog. Within that parameter, we can note the following possibilities:

- Sometimes the blessings are temporal and earthly, and at other times they are eschatological (to occur in the age to come).

- The blessings of the present age fall into a range of categories: material well-being, family blessings, national prosperity, and spiritual flourishing.
- Sometimes the blessings are conferred on the believing community, and sometimes on the righteous of the whole earth.
- An oracle of blessing belongs to a very large literary category known as a vision of the good life. An oracle of God's blessing is an ultimate vision of the good life—a standard toward which we should aspire. As we read multiple oracles of blessings, therefore, we can build a composite picture of the good life.

LEARNING BY DOING

The foregoing description has been brief, but it gives you what you need to make sense of an oracle of blessing. The following is a test case for you to analyze (Ezek. 34:25–30); the passage is an example of pastoral literature in which human experiences are portrayed under the metaphor of sheep:

> I will make with them a covenant of peace and banish wild beasts from the land, so that they may dwell securely in the wilderness and sleep in the woods. And I will make them and the places all around my hill a blessing, and I will send down the showers in their season; they shall be showers of blessing. And the trees of the field shall yield their fruit, and the earth shall yield its increase, and they shall be secure in their land. And they shall know that I am the LORD, when I break the bars of their yoke, and deliver them from the hand of those who enslaved them.

> They shall no more be a prey to the nations, nor shall the beasts of the land devour them. They shall dwell securely, and none shall make them afraid. And I will provide for them renowned plantations so that they shall no more be consumed with hunger in the land, and no longer suffer the reproach of the nations. And they shall know that I am the LORD their God with them, and that they, the house of Israel, are my people, declares the Lord GOD.

Oracle of Salvation

The oracle of salvation is also called the oracle of redemption. It often seems similar to the oracle of blessing, but usually we can note the following difference: the main element in an oracle of blessing is a catalog of blessings, whereas the oracle of salvation focuses on a change of fortune, situation, or relationship to God. The oracle of blessing is a static form compared to the explicit or implied change from disfavor with God to favor with God. Under the umbrella of the oracle of salvation, we can discern various categories, as the following discussion illustrates.

Change of Fortune

Some oracles of salvation are based on the premise of a change of fortune for the original recipients of the oracle. The change is from national catastrophe brought on as a punishment for rebelling against God's rules for living to prosperity. In terms of the historical context of these prophecies, the catastrophe consists of the predicted or actual defeat of Israel and Judah by invading armies. The pictures of restoration to prosperity cover a range of actual conditions, as we will see below. Here is an excerpt from a change-of-fortune oracle of salvation (Isa. 32:14–16):

For the palace is forsaken,
　　the populous city deserted;
the hill and the watchtower
　　will become dens forever,
a joy of wild donkeys,
　　a pasture of flocks;
until the Spirit is poured upon us from on high,
　　and the wilderness becomes a fruitful field,
　　and the fruitful field is deemed a forest.
Then justice will dwell in the wilderness,
　　and righteousness abide in the fruitful field.

This passage is a story of reversal from desolation to prosperity.

Change of Relationship to God

Whereas some oracles of salvation portray a reversal of fortune, others focus on the changed relationship between the recipients and God. Of course, this overlaps with the change-of-fortune oracles, but there is also a discernible difference, as seen in the following passage:

You shall no more be termed Forsaken,
　　and your land shall no more be termed Desolate,
but you shall be called My Delight Is in Her,
　　and your land Married;
for the LORD delights in you,
　　and your land shall be married. (Isa. 62:4)

This oracle announces a new state of favor with God after a state of disfavor brought on by rejection of God by his people (as portrayed in oracles of judgment).

Oracle of Restoration of the Jewish Nation after the Babylonian Captivity

The Old Testament prophets prophesied before and during the downfall of the kingdoms of Israel and Judah. We know that the kingdom of Judah spent seventy years in captivity, after which a remnant returned to Jerusalem and gradually resettled the land of Israel or Palestine (as narrated in the books of Ezra and Nehemiah). Some of the oracles of salvation predict the restoration of the nation in Palestine, as in the following passage:

> Thus says the LORD: In this place of which you say, "It is a waste without man or beast," in the cities of Judah and the streets of Jerusalem that are desolate, without man or inhabitant or beast, there shall be heard again the voice of mirth and the voice of gladness, the voice of the bridegroom and the voice of the bride, the voices of those who sing, as they bring thank offerings to the house of the LORD . . . For I will restore the fortunes of the land as at first, says the LORD. (Jer. 33:10–11)

We need to be on our guard against viewing too many of the oracles of salvation as having a short-term fulfillment in the return of the remnant, or at least against seeing *only* that dimension. Even when the details fit the return to Jerusalem, they can also be interpreted more symbolically or metaphorically and thereby receive a broader application. Here is a famous example:

> In that day I will raise up
> > the booth of David that is fallen
> and repair its breaches,
> > and raise up its ruins
> > and rebuild it as in the days of old. (Amos 9:11)

The architectural imagery certainly fits the description of the rebuilding of Jerusalem that we read about in the book of Nehemiah. But this is the very passage that was declared at the Council of Jerusalem in the book of Acts (15:16–17) as being fulfilled in the salvation of Gentiles, showing how metaphorically the prophetic oracle can be interpreted.

Salvation in Christ

Based on the foregoing, we can certainly interpret many of the oracles of salvation as pictures of what God achieves in the hearts and lives of those who trust in the atonement of Jesus for salvation. The picture of blessing that we find in these oracles is what Christians throughout history have experienced. The messianic prophecies will receive separate treatment in the following chapter, but they obviously belong to the category of oracles of salvation from sin and death through Christ. Other oracles of redemption also picture the reality of such salvation, with the following excerpt serving as an example:

> Comfort, comfort my people, says your God.
> Speak tenderly to Jerusalem,
>   and cry to her
> that her warfare is ended,
>   that her iniquity is pardoned. (Isa. 40:1–2a)

That is a picture of salvation as it exists for all believers, in all ages, though it is not incorrect to see it also as applying to the restored nation of God after the Babylonian captivity.

Salvation in the Age to Come

There is also an apocalyptic strand in the prophets' oracles of salvation. This means that the imagery fits best with pictures of the eternal salvation of believers and their glorification in heaven. The following is an example:

The sun shall be no more
  your light by day,
nor for brightness shall the moon
  give you light;
but the LORD will be your everlasting light,
  and your God will be your glory.
Your sun shall no more go down,
  nor your moon withdraw itself;
for the LORD will be your everlasting light,
  and your days of mourning shall be ended.
Your people shall all be righteous;
  they shall possess the land forever,
the branch of my planting, the work of my hands,
  that I might be glorified. (Isa. 60:19–21)

To summarize this unit on the oracle of salvation, it is obviously a very flexible form. It is an example of what literary scholars call "ambiguity," defined as something whose meaning could be either A or B, or something that can mean multiple things at the same time. Salvation emerges in these oracles as a wide-ranging spiritual reality.

LEARNING BY DOING

The following passage (Ezek. 37:21, 23–27) gives you an opportunity to apply the foregoing theory on the oracle of salvation:

Thus says the Lord GOD: Behold, I will take the people of Israel from the nations among which they have gone, and will gather them from all around, and bring them to their own land . . . They shall not defile themselves anymore with their idols and their detestable things, or with any of their transgressions. But I will save them from all the backslidings in which they have sinned, and will cleanse them; and they shall be my people, and I will be their God.

My servant David shall be king over them, and they shall all have one shepherd. They shall walk in my rules and be careful to obey my statutes. They shall dwell in the land that I gave to my servant Jacob, where your fathers lived. They and their children and their children's children shall dwell there forever, and David my servant shall be their prince forever. I will make a covenant of peace with them. It shall be an everlasting covenant with them. And I will set them in their land and multiply them, and will set my sanctuary in their midst forevermore. My dwelling place shall be with them, and I will be their God, and they shall be my people.

Relevance and Application

We cannot leave this chapter on the prophetic oracles without exploring the question of the relevance of Old Testament prophecy for us. The prophetic oracles are filled with references to specific situations of long ago. What is the relevance of a passage like the following?

Thus says the Lord GOD: Because Moab and Seir said, "Behold, the house of Judah is like all the other nations," therefore I will lay open the flank of Moab from the cities, from its cities on its frontier, the glory of the country, Beth–jeshimoth, Baal–meon, and Kiriathaim. I will give it along with the Ammonites to the people of the East as a possession, that the Ammonites may be remembered no more among the nations, and I will execute judgments upon Moab. Then they will know that I am the LORD. (Ezek. 25:8–11)

The surface details do not concern us at all. The relevance resides at the level of underlying principles. Literature is not only particularized and concrete, but also universal. Literary scholars call literature a "concrete universal." C. S. Lewis said that the particulars of literature are a net whereby the author captures the universal.

Applying this to the oracle of judgment quoted above, we can say that the character of God is still the same as portrayed in the oracle. God still punishes sin as he did with Moab and Seir. The implied warning embedded in the oracle is a warning to us also. The names have changed, but the spiritual principles remain the same. History tells us what *happened*, while literature tells us what *happens*. The prophetic books of the Bible tell us both, but the primary relevance for us resides in the universal message.

Our premise with every part of the Bible needs to be that "there is something here for me," no matter how remote the passage might be in its surface details. We can find relevance and application if we are patient and reflective. It is self-defeating to spend too much consecutive time in prophetic literature. I have found it helpful to alternate reading a chapter in a prophetic book with a chapter from elsewhere in the Bible.

Additional Prophetic Forms

Vision, Narrative, Symbolic Action, Taunt, Messianic Prophecy, and Colloquy

While oracles are the basic template of prophetic discourse, additional genres and literary forms and techniques find a place within that template. We can compare this to a genre like narrative. Within the overall category of narrative, numerous subgenres exist, such as hero story, tragedy, and travel story. In all instances, the smaller genres constitute an additional overlay of considerations both for the author and for us as interpreters. The literary forms that I am about to discuss do not negate what has been said about prophetic oracles but add further forms that we need to take into account.

Literary scholars apply the label "encyclopedic form" for texts that use an abundance of individual forms. Prophetic books are encyclopedic forms—collections of diverse individual elements. There is no attempt at narrative unity. The idea of a mixture of genres unifies an encyclopedic book.

This chapter discusses prophetic forms beyond oracles. A later chapter covers literary modes and genres shared by both prophecy and apocalypse, so this chapter does not complete the list of genres found in prophetic literature.

Prophetic Visions

The primary form of prophecy is an oracle or message from God, stated either directly or through the intermediary of a prophet. By contrast, the primary form of apocalyptic writing is not the oracle but the vision. But some prophetic passages come to us in the form of a vision rather than an oracle. One category of these is apocalyptic visions, which are discussed in a later chapter on apocalypse. But some visions are prophetic rather than apocalyptic in content.

The following is an example of a prophetic message that is phrased not in the familiar terms of what God *said* to the prophet but rather in terms of what he *showed* to the prophet (making it a vision): "This is what the Lord GOD showed me: behold, a basket of summer fruit" (Amos 8:1). God then interprets the vision for the prophet: "The end has come upon my people Israel" (v. 2).

This vision of Amos is a vision of judgment, but some of the prophetic visions are visions of blessing, or salvation. A particularly famous example is Ezekiel's vision of the valley of dry bones (Ezek. 37:1–14). The vision begins with the prophet's viewing a valley "full of bones," but as the prophet's dialogue with God unfolds, the bones become assembled into bodies with flesh. It is a vision of renewal, or new birth.

More generally, we can say that the prophetic books are filled with pictures. These are a form of vision, even when embedded in an oracle from God. The following passage (Isa. 33:8–9), for example, is a vision of a desolate land under God's judgment:

The highways lie waste;
    the traveler ceases.
Covenants are broken;
    cities are despised;
      there is no regard for man.
The land mourns and languishes;
    Lebanon is confounded and withers away;
Sharon is like a desert,
and Bashan and Carmel shake off their leaves.

A prophetic vision has a different format from a message announced as coming from God. Nonetheless, a vision of judgment or salvation does not require different analytic tools from what we use for an oracle of judgment or salvation. The questions provided as an analytic framework in the preceding chapter are the right ones to apply to a prophetic vision.

Prophetic Narrative

In addition to the oracles and visions that have been discussed thus far, the prophetic books also contain numerous narrative passages. The callings of Isaiah, Jeremiah, and Ezekiel all receive a full-fledged narrative account (Isaiah 6; Jeremiah 1; Ezekiel 1–3). There are numerous interspersed autobiographical narratives in the book of Jeremiah. We catch snatches of the lives of several prophets. For example, we learn that Hosea married an adulterous woman and reclaimed her as his wife after she had been faithless. Amos was a shepherd and dresser of sycamore figs before God called him to prophesy against Israel. Ezekiel lived in his own house, and his wife died in the middle of his prophetic ministry. Jeremiah was thrown into a cistern, and his rescuers threw down old clothes for Jeremiah to place between his armpits and ropes before being lifted up. And so forth.

We also read about external events. Isaiah 36–37 narrates the story of the invasion of Sennacherib, king of Assyria; his threatening letter to Hezekiah; and the defeat of his army by the angel of the Lord. Isaiah 38 tells the story of Hezekiah's recovery from illness. Jeremiah 36 narrates in leisurely detail the dramatic event of King Jehoiakim's cutting off segments from the scroll of Jeremiah's prophecy as it was read in his presence and burning the scroll piecemeal in the fire.

We are rarely induced to analyze these narrative segments according to the usual categories of plot, setting, and character. Nonetheless, we need to be aware of the interspersed narrative element in the prophetic books. There is action and personality as well as oracle and vision. We get to know the prophets. The narrative units also add a context into which the oracles and visions fit. When we finish reading a prophetic book, we feel that in some sense we have read a story.

Symbolic Actions

As an extension of the embedded stories in the prophetic books, some of these books contain narrative accounts of symbolic actions that the prophets were commanded by God to perform. On these occasions, the prophets *enacted* God's message instead of speaking it. The symbolic actions tend to be strange in the extreme. The following is a brief list of examples:

- Ezekiel cut his hair and disbursed it by thirds: he burned one-third of it, scattered one-third of it around the city, and threw one-third to the wind, saving a few hairs to bind in his robe, which he then burned (Ezek. 5:1–4).
- Jeremiah wore a wooden yoke on his neck and went about prophesying to his nation that Babylon would subdue it under its power as symbolized by the yoke (Jeremiah 27).

- Hosea married an adulteress woman and reclaimed her after she had left him (Hos. 1:2–3; 3:1–5). He named his children No Mercy and Not My People (1:6, 9).
- God commanded Isaiah to walk naked (in abbreviated clothing, surely) and barefoot for an extended period (Isa. 20:1–6).
- Ezekiel took a brick, engraved a city on it, and placed a siege wall around it (Ezek. 4:1–3).

That is only a *beginning* list!

How should we interpret such symbolic actions? We should treat them like any other symbol. We start by making sure we have the facts straight about the physical action. Then we need to analyze what is meant by the physical action. What is it a picture of? With the symbolic actions of the prophets, this is usually easy to determine because the account of the action is surrounded by commentary right in the text. For example, when Hosea reclaimed his wife, he explained to her that Israel, too, after a time of bondage, "shall return and seek the LORD their God" (Hos. 3:5). In other words, the history of Hosea's marriage has been a picture of the spiritual state of Israel, with apostasy followed by return to favor with God.

Taunt

We are prone to tame the Old Testament prophets beyond what the facts merit. In their day, the prophets were fringe figures within their own society. Their message and lifestyle tended to be extreme and out of the norm as they sought to capture the attention of a complacent society. If we imagine the prophets to be our neighbors, we would feel embarrassed to have them in the neighborhood. This is not uniformly the case, but it is true of most of the prophets. Just picture Ezekiel as your neighbor: after setting a siege wall around his brick (see above), he lay facing this "city under siege" on his left side for 390 days and then on his right side for 40 days, tied with cords so no one could turn him from one side to another (Ezek. 4:4–8).

I say the foregoing as a transition to my claim that the behavior and words of the prophets were not always "nice" or "refined." The prophets were capable of abrasive and scornful speech, and a literary form that embodies this is the taunt. The taunt was an important aspect of ancient life, especially in military contexts (though not limited to those contexts).

A taunt is an utterance that mocks or jeers an opponent. It is a put-down of an enemy. In our own common parlance, a taunt is a form of "trash talk." While the taunt can appear in any part of the Bible, our concern here is with the prophetic books. That the taunt is a major part of the prophetic milieu is suggested by Habakkuk 2:6a, where we read regarding the Babylonians, "Shall not all take up their taunt against him, with scoffing?"

Probably the most famous prophetic taunt is embedded in a narrative book, in the story of Elijah's duel with the prophets of Baal on Mount Carmel. When the prophets of Baal were unable to call down fire from heaven, Elijah (a prophet, we need to remember) uttered a formalized taunt that he composed impromptu:

And at noon [showdown at high noon, in effect] Elijah mocked them, saying, "Cry aloud, for he is a god. Either he is musing [thinking things through], or he is relieving himself [going to the toilet], or he is on a journey [out of the office], or perhaps he is asleep and must be awakened [needs a wake-up call]." (1 Kings 18:27)

In ancient cultures, such taunts were more than a form of mockery. They were regarded as carrying a genuine power, in effect being a weapon used in combat. We might think of them as a form of psychological warfare. This is suggested by Jeremiah 24:9, where God says, "I will make [the evil king and rulers of Judah] a horror to all the kingdoms of the earth, to be a reproach, a byword, a taunt, and a curse in all the places where I shall drive them." The taunt obviously keeps very bad company as it mingles with horror, reproach, byword, and curse.

We find snatches of taunt in scattered places throughout the prophetic books. Mere description of the downfall of a person or group does not count as a taunt. There needs to be an element of antagonism and put-down. The following excerpt from an oracle of judgment (Ezek. 5:13–16) has the requisite animosity to constitute a taunt:

> Thus shall my anger spend itself, and I will vent my fury upon them and satisfy myself. And they shall know that I am the LORD—that I have spoken in my jealousy—when I spend my fury upon them. Moreover, I will make you a desolation and an object of reproach among the nations all around you and in the sight of all who pass by. You shall be a reproach and a taunt, a warning and a horror, to the nations all around you, when I execute judgments on you in anger and fury, and with furious rebukes—I am the LORD; I have spoken—when I send against you the deadly arrows of famine, arrows for destruction, which I will send to destroy you, and when I bring more and more famine upon you and break your supply of bread.

A modern counterpart might be to say to an opponent who has wronged us, "You'll get yours" (i.e., "your due punishment"). To say "you'll get yours" is not simply to make a prediction but to express hostility.

The foregoing discussion has covered snatches of taunting in the prophetic books. We should not overstate the presence of these passages in the prophets, nor should we understate it. The denunciation of evil and prediction of God's punishment of it is delineated in such minute detail that the prophets' message is constantly drifting in the direction of a taunt. Perhaps we can gain a perspective by imagining that our own doom was being predicted in these pictures. We would experience the prediction as a taunt, and our feelings would be hurt.

In addition to this general spirit that borders on taunting, we find more extended passages of taunting. The literary term for this genre is "taunt song." It is a somewhat formal and ritualized unit, as the prophet sticks with the delineation of an evil person or group getting its comeuppance. Chapter 2 of Habakkuk is commonly regarded as a collection of taunt songs. Here is an excerpt:

> You will have your fill of shame instead of glory.
> > Drink, yourself, and show your uncircumcision!
> The cup in the LORD's right hand
> > will come around to you,
> > and utter shame will come upon your glory!
> The violence done to Lebanon will overwhelm you,
> > as will the destruction of the beasts that terrified them,
> for the blood of man and violence to the earth,
> > to cities and all who dwell in them. (vv. 16–17)

The first tip-off that this is more than an ordinary oracle of judgment is the direct address to the nation of Babylon. There is an element of personal attack, not simply a general description of what will happen, and the prophet "rubs it in."

Messianic Prophecy

An important prophetic form is the messianic prophecy that predicts the coming of the Christ, the Messiah. If we compile these prophecies into a composite story, they cover the entire earthly life of Jesus—his birth, his teachings and miracles, his atoning death, his resurrection, and his ascension. Most of these Old Testament prophecies are referenced in the Gospels and Epistles in connection with their fulfillment in the life of Christ. The following is an example of a messianic prophecy (Isa. 9:6–7):

> For to us a child is born,
>   to us a son is given;
> and the government shall be upon his shoulder,
>   and his name shall be called
> Wonderful Counselor, Mighty God,
>   Everlasting Father, Prince of Peace.
> Of the increase of his government and of peace
>   there will be no end,
> on the throne of David and over his kingdom,
>   to establish it and to uphold it
> with justice and with righteousness
>   from this time forth and forevermore.

Prophetic Colloquy

As we read the prophetic books, we are constantly aware that God is speaking to people. This so dominates our impression that we can easily overlook that not everything in the prophetic books is coming down from God; there are also interspersed passages in which the prophet speaks to God or responds to what God has said. The literary term for this form is "colloquy."

In this context, colloquy means "response, reaction, conversation, dialog." The devotional poetry of John Donne and George Herbert provides a useful example. Donne and Herbert modeled many of their devotional poems on a medieval tradition of contemplation. The format consisted of three parts: (1) imagining oneself present at an event from the Bible ("composing the scene," according to the handbooks); (2) meditating on the event; (3) prayer of response ("colloquy"). The prophetic colloquy in which the prophet responds to a message from God is an important genre in the prophetic books.

The book of Jeremiah contains a higher number of colloquies than other prophetic books do. An example is the following, which the prophet adds after an oracle of judgment:

Heal me, O LORD, and I shall be healed;
    save me, and I shall be saved,
      for you are my praise. (17:14)

The book of Micah ends with a colloquy that begins with these words of response:

Who is a God like you, pardoning iniquity
    and passing over transgression
      for the remnant of his inheritance?
He does not retain his anger forever,
    because he delights in steadfast love. (7:18)

A certain range exists within the general format of the prophet's response to God. Some colloquies are in the nature of a personal testimony. The conclusion of the book of Habakkuk is a famous example. It reads in part:

Though the fig tree should not blossom,
    nor fruit be on the vines,
the produce of the olive fail
    and the fields yield no food,
the flock be cut off from the fold,
    and there be no herd in the stalls,
yet I will rejoice in the LORD;
    I will take joy in the God of my salvation. (3:17–18)

Some of the prophetic colloquies resemble lyric poems, expressing the heightened thoughts and feelings of a poet. This is not surprising, inasmuch as lyric is preeminently the poet's response to a stimulus. The following passage (Isa. 40:28–29) is an excerpt from a poem that is not ascribed to God and that can therefore be read as a praise psalm that expresses the prophet's response, perhaps addressed to an implied listener:

Have you not known? Have you not heard?
The LORD is the everlasting God,
   the Creator of the ends of the earth.
He does not faint or grow weary;
   his understanding is unsearchable.
He gives power to the faint,
   and to him who has no might he increases strength.

At this point we can draw a helpful comparison to the book of Psalms. The two main types of psalms are the praise psalm and the lament psalm. Those categories are common in the prophetic colloquies as well. The passage quoted immediately above is a praise psalm. The entire book of Lamentations can be considered as a lament that expresses the prophet's grief over the fall of Jerusalem. Here is an excerpt:

I am the man who has seen affliction,
   under the rod of his wrath;
he has driven and brought me
   into darkness without any light. (3:1–2)

What interpretive rules apply to the prophetic colloquies? First, note them and label them as expressing the prophet's response. They are not a message from God. I find that I tend to read nearly everything in the prophetic books as though it is an oracle from God, not shifting gears as I should when I come to a colloquy. Second, a colloquy can be analyzed approximately as we analyze a lyric poem: dominant theme or motif, method by which the author develops that theme, and overall mood. Having analyzed a colloquy as it is in itself, we should relate it to its preceding context since a colloquy is a response to God's message, in the mode of a dialog or conversation.

LEARNING BY DOING

This chapter has covered six prophetic genres: vision, narrative, symbolic action, taunt, messianic prophecy, and colloquy. The following six passages represent these genres, but they are not listed in the order followed earlier in this chapter. Use your own Bible to find the passages:

- Isaiah 14:12–17
- Jeremiah 10:23–25
- Isaiah 53:4–9
- Jeremiah 13:1–11
- Jeremiah 38:7-13
- Daniel 8:1-4

Satire

I expect that it will raise some eyebrows to see a chapter on satire in a book on prophetic and apocalyptic literature. Nonetheless, this inclusion is entirely defensible, and to omit it would leave a major gap. I note in passing that satire is not a continuous presence only in prophetic and apocalyptic literature; it makes an appearance in all parts of the Bible. To master the genre of satire as I present it in this chapter can yield dividends for reading and teaching the entire Bible.

Defining Satire

Satire is an attack on human vice or folly. The reliable tip-off that a passage is satiric is the presence of an object of attack or exposure. Since many people assume that comedy or humor is an indispensable part of satire, let me decisively dissociate satire from humor. The book of Amos is a full-fledged satire, and it does not contain anything laughable. A stronger case can be made for ridicule as a feature of satire, but even here there are exceptions.

Satire is built around these four ingredients:

- One or more objects of attack.
- A satiric vehicle in which the attack is embodied. Narrative or story is a common satiric vehicle, but probably only half of the satire in the Bible and the world generally is enshrined in a story. Compiling a satiric portrait is a common strategy. A catalog of vices might fit the need. Direct denunciation is common, as when a prophet says, "Woe to . . ."
- A satiric norm. As used in this situation, a norm is a standard. A satiric norm is the standard of correctness by which an object of attack is judged. In the Bible, the satiric norm is the guidelines for living that God has imposed on the human race.
- The satiric tone. Tone refers to the author's attitude toward his material. If we view it from the reader's point of view, we are talking about the mood or spirit that the work creates. There are two possible satiric tones—light and laughing, or sharp and biting. The one aims to *laugh* vice out of existence, and the other to *lash* vice out of existence.

The following passage, which recounts an imaginary event in the prophet Ezekiel's life (Ezek. 8:7–12), is an example of satire:

And he [a form that had the appearance of a man] brought me to the entrance of the court, and when I looked, behold, there was a hole in the wall. Then he said to me, "Son of man, dig in the wall." So I dug in the wall, and behold, there was an entrance. And he said to me, "Go in, and see the vile abominations that they are committing here." So I went in and saw. And there, engraved on the wall all around, was every form of creeping things and loathsome beasts, and all the idols of the house of Israel. And before them stood seventy men of the elders of the house of Israel, with Jaazaniah the son of Shaphan standing among them. Each had his censer in his hand, and the smoke of the cloud of incense went up. Then he said to me, "Son of man, have you seen what the elders of the house of Israel are doing in the dark, each in his room of pictures? For they say, 'The LORD does not see us, the LORD has forsaken the land.'"

If we apply the satiric framework to this passage, we have the following:

- Object of attack: the religious establishment of Israel, but probably the elders represent the entire religious community. More specifically, the elders are guilty of idolatry, and that, in turn, may cover their rebellion against God more generally.
- Satiric vehicle: a vision. Further literary techniques cluster in the passage, however. There is an overall narrative framework, so it is accurate to speak of narrative as a satiric vehicle in this passage (which we remember as a story) of what Ezekiel did and saw. The story is not simply fictional but has touches of fantasy. A summary statement is that the satiric vehicle is a fantasy story reported as a vision.
- Satiric norm: by inference, the true worship of God and obedience to him. As we watch the elders go through their perverted worship of God by worshiping idols, we are fully aware that they should be worshiping God and giving him their obedience. We are conscious of witnessing a perversion of what should be.
- Satiric tone: serious and heavy. We shudder as we see elders worshiping idols in the temple.

The Oracle of Judgment as Satire

The first application of satire to prophecy and apocalypse is thus to freestanding satiric passages like Ezekiel's vision of the elders in the temple. The second application is to the oracles of judgment, which are the most numerous category of oracles. We will do a better job of interacting with an oracle of judgment if we have the satiric framework in mind. Some oracles of judgment are complete satires, while others simply have affinities to certain aspects of satire.

Zechariah 5:1–4 illustrates how an oracle of judgment can be a satire:

> Again I lifted my eyes and saw, and behold, a flying scroll! And he [an angel] said to me, "What do you see?" I answered, "I see a flying scroll. Its length is twenty cubits [60 feet], and its width ten cubits [30 feet]." Then he said to me, "This is the curse that goes out over the face of the whole land. For everyone who steals shall be cleaned out according to what is on one side, and everyone who swears falsely shall be cleaned out according to what is on the other side. I will send it out, declares the LORD of hosts, and it shall enter the house of the thief, and the house of him who swears falsely by my name. And it shall remain in his house and consume it, both timber and stones."

Application of the satiric framework yields the following results:

- Objects of attack: stealing and lying.
- Satiric vehicles: imaginary vision; fantasy; narrative.
- Satiric norm: from the fact that God will administer punishment we can infer that the character and commands of God are the standard by which guilty people (the objects of attack) are found lacking.
- Satiric tone: serious, evoking a sense of fear.

The satiric framework gives us a method for being analytic with an oracle of judgment. It also makes sure that we are thorough in our analysis of it.

The Book of Amos

The book of Amos would by itself justify a chapter on satire. No one would question that the book of Amos is a prophetic book that bears all of the traits of that genre. Yet it is so thoroughly a book of satire that when I teach it, I do so in a unit on satire. While I *could* apply the criteria of prophetic literature to the book, to do so seems extraneous to the kind of book it primarily is.

I begin with the book as a whole, in an awareness that the individual parts are a series of satiric units within the whole. The object of attack is national, institutional, and group evil. At the broadest level, the book of Amos is an exposé of the evils of a whole society (the nation of Israel and in chapters 1–2 neighboring countries as well). Within that parameter, certain institutions are exposed. One is the religious establishment, chiefly the priesthood. Another is governmental structures such as the judicial and military systems. Additionally, Amos attacks the wealthy and privileged class and religious hypocrites who live self-centered lives. Corporate or communal evil is the subject of Amos.

The satiric vehicles for Amos's satire are extremely varied. In fact, this short book is very nearly a compendium of leading prophetic forms. Oracles of judgment dominate, but the book ends with an oracle of salvation in the form of a vision of a coming golden age (9:11–15). That passage can legitimately be read as a prophecy of restoration after captivity and the blessings of the messianic age, and an apocalyptic vision of eternal life in eternity. There are visions in addition to oracles; there is a doom song. This is only a beginning list, but it suffices for our purposes here.

The satiric norm is the character of God and his commands for people. A passage such as the following offers an example:

> Seek good, and not evil,
>> that you may live;
> and so the LORD, the God of hosts, will be with you,
>> as you have said. (5:14)

In the same vein are commands to "seek me and live" (5:4) and "seek the LORD and live" (5:6). Seeking and obeying God is the satiric norm by which the behavior of sinful nations and people is measured.

The satiric tone of Amos is uniformly sharp and biting. There is no bantering from this prophet, who is the type of social activist we can imagine leading a protest.

LEARNING BY DOING

The following passage from Amos (6:1–8) is part of an oracle of judgment against Israel. It will enable you to apply what has been said above about prophetic oracles.

> "Woe to those who are at ease in Zion,
> and to those who feel secure on the mountain of Samaria,
> the notable men of the first of the nations,
>> to whom the house of Israel comes!
> Pass over to Calneh, and see,
>> and from there go to Hamath the great;
>> then go down to Gath of the Philistines.
> Are you better than these kingdoms?
>> Or is their territory greater than your territory,

O you who put far away the day of disaster
   and bring near the seat of violence?
Woe to those who lie on beds of ivory
   and stretch themselves out on their couches,
and eat lambs from the flock
   and calves from the midst of the stall,
who sing idle songs to the sound of the harp
   and like David invent for themselves instruments of music,
who drink wine in bowls
   and anoint themselves with the finest oils,
   but are not grieved over the ruin of Joseph!
Therefore they shall now be the first of those who go into exile,
   and the revelry of those who stretch themselves out shall pass away."
The Lord GOD has sworn by himself, declares the LORD, the God of hosts:
   "I abhor the pride of Jacob
      and hate his strongholds,
      and I will deliver up the city and all that is in it."

Apocalyptic Satire

Vast parts of the prophetic books are satiric. The same cannot be said of the apocalyptic parts of the Bible. Yet satire is important in them too. For starters, the detailed portrayal of the spread of evil and natural disaster that we find in apocalyptic visions is an implied picture of God's judgment on sinful humanity. Knowing that, we can pick up clues as to why God is punishing humanity, and also what the human race has done to bring this punishment on itself. These clues of bad behavior are an implied satiric attack on people, who are being punished for specific things that they have done.

In a related way, the fact that God is the one who is handing out punishment leads us to infer that God and his rules for living are the satiric norm. The people who are punished (either now or in an apocalyptic future) are guilty of sin against God. This is an inference, but once we are aware of it, we can fit the details into an overall satiric design.

The following excerpt from the letter to the church in Sardis (Rev. 3:1–5) typifies the interspersed satiric interludes in apocalyptic literature:

And to the angel of the church in Sardis write: "The words of him [Christ] who has the seven spirits of God and the seven stars.

"I know your works. You have the reputation of being alive, but you are dead. Wake up, and strengthen what remains and is about to die, for I have not found your works complete in the sight of my God. Remember, then, what you received and heard. Keep it, and repent. If you will not wake up, I will come like a thief, and you will not know at what hour I will come against you. Yet you have still a few names in Sardis, people who have not soiled their garments, and they will walk with me in white, for they are worthy. The one who conquers will be clothed thus in white garments, and I will never blot his name out of the book of life. I will confess his name before my Father and before his angels."

The satire works itself out in the following way:

- Object of attack: spiritual deadness.
- Satiric vehicle: a letter in which Christ makes an accusation and issues a warning to the church at Sardis; a diagnosis of the spiritual state of that church.
- Satiric norm: being spiritually alive. The passage is constructed as a contrast, with the spiritually dead (object of attack) being contrasted to the "few" who are spiritually alive (the satiric norm).
- Satiric tone: serious.

The apocalyptic visions of the Bible are not as continuously satiric as the prophetic books, but the dynamics of satire (object of attack, vehicle, norm, tone) are almost constantly at work and can be applied accordingly. Another way of saying this is that, while apocalyptic writing does not require application of the satiric framework, it is certain to illuminate the text we are studying at any given moment.

LEARNING BY DOING

Revelation 18:4–8 is a passage of satire that will enable you to apply what this chapter has covered:

Then I heard another voice from heaven saying,
"Come out of her, my people,
   lest you take part in her sins,
lest you share in her plagues;
for her sins are heaped high as heaven,
   and God has remembered her iniquities.
Pay her back as she herself has paid back others,
   and repay her double for her deeds;

> mix a double portion for her in the cup she mixed.
> As she glorified herself and lived in luxury,
>> so give her a like measure of torment and mourning,
> since in her heart she says,
>> 'I sit as a queen,
> I am no widow,
>> and mourning I shall never see.'
> For this reason her plagues will come in a single day,
>> death and mourning and famine,
> and she will be burned up with fire;
>> for mighty is the Lord God who has judged her."

The Rhetoric of Ridicule and Sarcasm

This section appears here because I did not know where else to put it in this guide. I began this chapter by dissociating satire from humor as a necessary ingredient, but satire beyond the Bible has often been comic satire. Even though ridicule is not always present in satire, in the Bible it often is, and this concluding section is designed to alert my readers to it.

When we ridicule something or someone, we dismiss them and make them appear foolish or contemptible. Ridicule consists of laying out human failing to full view, in such a way as to instill rejection of it and perhaps contempt for it. A prominent satiric genre in prophetic literature is the ridicule of idol worshipers by portraying the folly of carving a lifeless idol and then worshiping it. Out of numerous examples, I offer the following excerpt:

"For the customs of the peoples are vanity.
A tree from the forest is cut down
   and worked with an axe by the hands of a craftsman.

They decorate it with silver and gold;
>they fasten it with hammer and nails
>so that it cannot move.
Their idols are like scarecrows in a cucumber field,
>and they cannot speak;
they have to be carried,
>for they cannot walk.
Do not be afraid of them,
>for they cannot do evil,
>neither is it in them to do good."
There is none like you, O LORD;
>you are great, and your name is great in might.
Who would not fear you, O King of the nations?
>For this is your due;
for among all the wise ones of the nations
>and in all their kingdoms
>there is none like you.
They are both stupid and foolish;
>the instruction of idols is but wood! (Jer. 10:3–8)

Ridicule is a form of mockery, and in this passage idol worshipers are mocked.

The foregoing idol passage is an extended work of ridicule. But a statement of ridicule can be a one-line put-down. Amos addresses the wealthy women of Jerusalem as "you cows of Bashan" (4:1). The priestly exhortation to the people was, "Come to Bethel, and worship"; Amos twists it to say, "Come to Bethel, and transgress" (4:4). Sarcasm leaks out when Amos, after describing people's coming to make sacrifices and pay vows, adds, "For so you love to do, O people of Israel!"(4:5). Isaiah pictures pagan mediums and necromancers as people "who chirp and mutter" (8:19).

As a final example I offer the following picture that Isaiah paints of proud women, making no attempt whatever to conceal his contempt for what he portrays:

> The LORD said:
> Because the daughters of Zion are haughty
>   and walk with outstretched necks,
>   glancing wantonly with their eyes,
> mincing along as they go,
>   tinkling with their feet (3:16)

The description is handled in such a way as to render the women ridiculous.

What are we to make of prophetic ridicule and sarcasm? It matches the image we have of a prophet. A prophet's task is not to compliment people and make them feel good about how they are conducting their lives. We expect prophets to denounce and rebuke, and are not surprised if they are abrasive.

Visionary Literature

P art of the complexity of the parts of the Bible covered in this guide is the overlapping nature of the main categories. Prophetic writing is sometimes apocalyptic. Parts of the apocalyptic visions of the Bible read like prophecy. Topping that is the amorphous category of visionary writing. Literary scholars use the label "mode" to name literary forms that can appear in a whole range of genres. Visionary writing is a literary mode.

We need to start with the continuum that makes up literature as a whole. At one end is realism, based on the premise of verisimilitude (lifelikeness). It aims to reproduce the reality of the physical and human world as we know it. At the other end of the continuum is fantasy, which transports us to an alternate reality and strange world. Visionary literature exists at this end of the continuum.

The purpose of this chapter is to examine the features that make up visionary writing. I have placed the chapter after the one on prophetic literature because visionary techniques are less continuously present in prophetic literature than other features.

By contrast, visionary literature is the dominant mode of apocalyptic literature. This chapter serves as a preamble to apocalyptic writing. We need to understand the visionary mode before we can navigate apocalyptic writing. Just as poetry (a form of discourse) is the material out of which poems are made, visionary writing is the "air" in which apocalyptic writers live and move and have their being.

The game plan for this chapter is to break the visionary mode into constituent parts and illustrate each one. A quick listing of all the features of visionary literature would leave us with a superficial understanding of it, so we need to examine the individual parts in detail.

Before we look at individual visionary techniques, though, we need an overarching definition of the concept "visionary." For starters, if something is visionary, it is *merely imagined,* or *envisioned.* In our world it does not exist empirically (physically, actually, experientially). It is like a dream or vision in not being tangible and actual (or perhaps even possible) in the world around us. Dragons who sweep down stars with their tails exist only in our imagination. They are envisioned rather than actual.

Prophetic Poetry as a Form of Visionary Literature

Poetry is inherently fictional and often fantastic. We might say that poets are always playing a game of make-believe, telling us things that we know to be literally false. At the time of the exodus, the mountains did not literally skip like rams (Ps. 114:4). Epidemic illness is not actually a stalker (Ps. 91:6). Believing in Jesus as Savior does not literally entail opening a door and eating a meal with Jesus (Rev. 3:20). I am fond of a book on poetry that bears a chapter with the title "The Making of Unreality."

While this poetic game of make-believe characterizes poetry as a whole, in some of the poetry of the prophetic books the making of unreality is more extreme than what we find in poetry generally. Prophetic poetry often has a certain daring quality that makes it a category of visionary writing.

To metaphorically portray a military defeat as "a day of clouds and thick darkness" (Zeph. 1:15) is within the normal range of poetic license. By contrast, it ranks as "extreme poetry" to personify a nation and then proceed to portray its military defeat as having its head shaved with a razor, "the head and the hair of the feet, and it will sweep away the beard also" (Isa. 7:20). Poets from time immemorial have portrayed terrified people as shaking with fear, but prophets take it a step further when they say that "every human heart will melt" and people will "look aghast at one another" with "their faces aflame" (Isa. 13:7–8). It is within the norm for ordinary poetry to picture a wayward people as wandering sheep (Isa. 53:6), whereas the following prophetic passage takes it to the next level:

> [people] who sit in tombs,
>   and spend the night in secret places;
> who eat pig's flesh,
>   and broth of tainted meat is in their vessels. (Isa. 65:4)

There is a certain "above and beyond" quality in much of the poetry in the prophets. This is admittedly subjective. But at least we can say that the poetry of the prophets keeps us rather continuously in a world that is merely envisioned, not resembling daily reality. What are we to make of this? It is the task of the prophet to challenge complacency. Part of that challenge consists of confronting us with an alternate reality to our familiar routine.

The Strange World Motif

A preliminary point that I need to make is that for the remainder of this chapter I will make no distinction between prophetic literature and apocalyptic writing. They both share the qualities that make up the visionary mode. Apocalypse makes more continuous use of visionary techniques, whereas the prophets consistently have an eye on the contemporary scene. Nonetheless, prophetic writing makes intermittent use of visionary techniques.

Worldmaking is an essential skill required of the composer of visionary literature. In contrast to the familiar world evoked by a realist, the visionary world is what literary scholars call "a strange world." It is equally accurate to speak of the element of "otherness," and the adjective "otherworldly" is a common designation. Visionary literature transports us to another, merely imagined world. To get a handle on this, we can use the familiar categories of any literary world, consisting of setting, characters, and actions.

The setting of a visionary realm is not *entirely* strange. If it were, we would not be able to grasp it. The settings of visionary worlds are a combination of the real and the fantastic. The opening scene in the story of the call of Isaiah (Isa. 6:1–2) offers a perfect example:

> In the year that King Uzziah died I saw the LORD sitting upon a throne, high and lifted up, and the train of his robe filled the temple. Above him stood the seraphim. Each had six wings: with two he covered his face, and with two he covered his feet, and with two he flew.

Even today we can picture a throne room, so we start with our feet on the ground. To say that God is "high and lifted up" introduces the first element of "otherness": *how* high and *how* lifted up? There is an element of mystery in the description. How can a robe fill an entire temple? And how did we move from a throne room to a temple? As for the seraphim, they defy all realistic images we have from the known world. The transcendent scene of Isaiah's call transports us to a strange world.

Many of the visionary settings in the prophetic and apocalyptic books are adaptations of the world of nature, and as such less extreme than Isaiah's vision of God. Here is an example:

> I looked on the earth, and behold, it was without form and void;
> and to the heavens, and they had no light.
> I looked on the mountains, and behold, they were quaking,
> and all the hills moved to and fro. (Jer. 4:23–24)

The individual objects are all familiar to us, but the composite scene of these details is so strange that we cannot picture it. We have been transported to another world. Again, we are familiar with mountains, but not mountains of bronze (Zech. 6:1).

The strange settings of visionary literature are populated partly by strange beings. Some of them are supernatural agents like angels and seraphim and heavenly armies. The horses in John's vision of the four horsemen (Rev. 6:1–8) are colored white, bright red, black, and pale (literally yellowish-green). Zechariah saw two women who had wings like a stork (5:9).

A large category of visionary agents is animals who behave like people, as in the horses of John's vision that have serpentine tails and fire and smoke coming out of their mouths and that attack people as though they were warriors (Rev. 9:18–19). The killer locusts of Joel's prophecy are a particularly famous example:

> Their appearance is like the appearance of horses,
> and like war horses they run.
> As with the rumbling of chariots,
> they leap on the tops of the mountains,
> like the crackling of a flame of fire
> devouring the stubble,
> like a powerful army
> drawn up for battle. (2:4–5)

These visionary creatures illustrate the fantastic, "over the top" quality of prophetic poetry discussed earlier.

Yet another category is forces of nature that act as characters in a story. In the following excerpt from Jesus' Olivet Discourse, the heavenly bodies are portrayed as actors in the final eschaton (climax of history):

> Immediately after the tribulation of those days the sun will be darkened, and the moon will not give its light, and the stars will fall from heaven, and the powers of the heavens will be shaken. (Matt. 24:29)

If the settings and characters of visionary literature are a combination of the real and fantastic, so are the events that happen. We read about such impossible events as the earth being "shaken out of its place" (Isa. 13:13), a river overflowing an entire land and reaching neck-level in depth (Isa. 8:8), and four cherubim who move through the air in coordinated formation accompanied by whirling wheels (Ezek. 10:9–14). Events like this do not happen in real life, but they are the very stuff out of which visionary literature is made.

LEARNING BY DOING

The foregoing unit has delineated how visionary literature transports us to a strange world. The following excerpt from Ezekiel's vision of the divine chariot will enable you to identify the specific features of the world that the author has created (with setting, character or agent, and event constituting the vocabulary):

> As I looked, behold, a stormy wind came out of the north, and a great cloud, with brightness around it, and fire flashing forth continually, and in the midst of the fire, as it were gleaming metal. And from the midst of it came the like-

ness of four living creatures. And this was their appearance: they had a human likeness, but each had four faces, and each of them had four wings. Their legs were straight, and the soles of their feet were like the sole of a calf's foot. And they sparkled like burnished bronze. Under their wings on their four sides they had human hands. And the four had their faces and their wings thus: their wings touched one another. Each one of them went straight forward, without turning as they went. As for the likeness of their faces, each had a human face. The four had the face of a lion on the right side, the four had the face of an ox on the left side, and the four had the face of an eagle. Such were their faces. And their wings were spread out above. Each creature had two wings, each of which touched the wing of another, while two covered their bodies. And each went straight forward. Wherever the spirit would go, they went, without turning as they went. As for the likeness of the living creatures, their appearance was like burning coals of fire, like the appearance of torches moving to and fro among the living creatures. And the fire was bright, and out of the fire went forth lightning. And the living creatures darted to and fro, like the appearance of a flash of lightning. (Ezek. 1:4–14)

Temporal Reversal and Transformation

The strange worlds of visionary literature transport us physically (though in our imagination rather than literally). But visionary writing is as likely to transport us temporally. The strategy here is to keep us rooted in the world of reality, but to project the time forward. In such visions, conditions are drastically altered from the present moment. As we read the account, we are again transported to a world that is merely *envisioned* and not yet operative. In the envisioned transformation, the altered conditions in the future are usually as strange as the "other" worlds discussed in the preceding unit.

Most of the futuristic prophecies of the prophetic books are based on the premise of reversal as described in the preceding paragraph. Three chapters dealing with the kingdom of Tyre in the middle of Ezekiel provide a memorable example. At the time of Ezekiel's prophecy, Tyre was at its height, the envy of the world. Ezekiel 27:1–25 paints a dazzling picture of Tyre's prosperity. With that picture of the present moment before us, Ezekiel's vision of future destruction is an example of an *envisioned* reality that would have seemed unreal to people at the time of Ezekiel's prophecy. Here is an excerpt:

> [The armies of Nebuchadnezzar] shall destroy the walls of Tyre and break down her towers, and I will scrape her soil from her and make her a bare rock. She shall be in the midst of the sea a place for the spreading of nets, for I have spoken, declares the Lord GOD. And she shall become plunder for the nations, and her daughters on the mainland shall be killed by the sword. Then they will know that I am the LORD.

> For thus says the Lord GOD: Behold, I will bring against Tyre from the north Nebuchadnezzar king of Babylon, king of kings, with horses and chariots, and with horsemen and a host of many soldiers. He will kill with the sword your daughters on the mainland. He will set up a siege wall against you and throw up a mound against you, and raise a roof of shields against you. (26:4–8)

For contemporaries of Ezekiel, the vision of future ruin would have seemed as farfetched as a fantasy movie might seem today.

A variation on the basic paradigm occurs when the temporal contrast is between past and present. Strictly speaking this does meet the criterion of being an *envisioned* time, but in other ways the effect is so similar to visions of the altered future that they can be included under the visionary umbrella. Here is an example:

> Her princes were purer than snow,
> > whiter than milk;
> their bodies were more ruddy than coral,
> > the beauty of their form was like sapphire.
> Now their face is blacker than soot;
> > they are not recognized in the streets;
> their skin has shriveled on their bones;
> > it has become as dry as wood. (Lam. 4:7–8)

As in the prophecies that predict a change of fortune in the future, this portrait of an already-defeated Jerusalem is based on the premise of a stark reversal.

Interpreting Visionary Literature

What are the ground rules for reading and interpreting the strange worlds of the visionary imagination? Our first task is to open ourselves to the wonder, mystery, and otherness of the venture. For people who have antennae only for literary realism, the apocalyptic parts of the Bible will remain a closed book. As we read the Bible, there are times to have our feet firmly planted in the ground (historical realism), and there are times to let our imaginations soar (visionary literature). At the broadest possible level, visionary literature intends to jolt us out of our complacent assumption that earthly reality in its current form is the only reality that exists. Additionally, the Bible is a book for all temperaments and mental types. Fantasy appeals to one segment of the human race, and its presence in the Bible signals that God wants it to appeal to everyone.

Literary scholars speak of the ability of literature to defamiliarize experience—the ability to present experience and reality in a way that we will take note when the dull routine of life has numbed us to see reality. All literature has this ability to some degree, but visionary literature specializes in it. If a prophet were to say that a foreign army is going to invade a land, it would be a ho-hum statement, but the picture of a river overflowing a country grabs our attention.

Additionally, we can say that visionary writing embodies and expresses some realities and experiences better than any other form can. For example, supernatural reality is just that—beyond the natural. The "otherness" of visionary writing captures that quality. Apocalyptic literature portrays unprecedented forms of terror; visionary scenes like the sea becoming blood embody this unprecedented horror in a way that prosaic scenes from everyday life do not.

Then, too, no matter how remote the details of visionary literature seem compared to everyday life, the unlifelike details nonetheless portray realities. The ability of visionary literature to express truth and delineate life in the world is not in doubt. We simply need to know how to connect the vision to life. Samuel Johnson, man of letters in the eighteenth century, said regarding fiction that we do not mistake its details for real life, but those details *bring real life to mind*. I am claiming the same thing for visionary writing in the Bible.

In the introduction to this guide I claimed that one of the things that makes prophecy and apocalypse intimidating to us is the need to find the referent—the truth or reality to which the details in the text point. This is not as difficult as we think. Usually the text itself gives us what we need. I do not have space here to analyze a complex passage like the four-horse visions in Revelation, so I will take a simple example: Ezekiel's vision of a divine chariot (Ezekiel 1, excerpted earlier in this chapter). What does this dazzling and bewildering collection of details portray? It portrays the glory of God. An abstraction like "God is glorious" does not pack the punch that Ezekiel's vision does.

I do not mean to imply that all visionary passages carry their interpretive keys within the text. In some cases, we have no good alternative but to consult a study Bible or commentary. But our own hunches and intuitions are often reliable. For example, we do not need to consult an expert to conclude that a male child "who is to rule all the nations with a rod of iron" (Rev. 12:5) is Christ, and that the sun and moon being darkened (Joel 3:15 and many other places in apocalyptic writing) is a picture of the end of human history.

An additional principle is that literature combines the concrete (particular) with the universal. This means that although characters in a story certainly represent themselves, they also embody what is true for all people. What happens to them is specific, but they are examples of what happens to us too. The same is true of visions. A vision of judgment against a specific king or nation embodies the principle of God's judgment against evil that applies to us too.

My final point is that one of the functions and effects of visionary literature is to create a sense of supernatural reality. By definition, supernatural reality transcends earthly reality. It is spiritual, and we live in a physical world. Visionary literature exists to open windows onto the unseen spiritual world. That world contains much that is mysterious to us. If this is the case, not everything in visionary literature can be explained. We need to accept some of it as simply assuring us that a supernatural realm exists. This is not the *whole* story, as the preceding paragraphs indicate.

LEARNING BY DOING

This chapter has covered three main topics: the strange world motif (the other worlds of visionary literature), temporal reversal as a form of alternate reality to what currently prevails, and ground rules for interacting with visionary literature and interpreting what the details and visions mean. The following passage (Zechariah 5) dispenses with temporal reversal as a visionary technique but the passage will enable you to apply what was covered in the rest of the chapter.

Again I lifted my eyes and saw, and behold, a flying scroll! And he [an angel] said to me, "What do you see?" I answered, "I see a flying scroll. Its length is twenty cubits [60 feet], and its width ten cubits [30 feet]." Then he said to me, "This is the curse that goes out over the face of the whole land. For everyone who steals shall be cleaned out according to what is on one side, and everyone who swears falsely shall be cleaned out according to what is on the other side. I will send it out, declares the LORD of hosts, and it shall enter the house of the thief, and the house of him who swears falsely by my name. And it shall remain in his house and consume it, both timber and stones."

Then the angel who talked with me came forward and said to me, "Lift your eyes and see what this is that is going out." And I said, "What is it?" He said, "This is the basket that is going out." And he said, "This is their iniquity in all the land." And behold, the leaden cover was lifted, and there was a woman sitting in the basket! And he said, "This is Wickedness." And he thrust her back into the basket, and thrust down the leaden weight on its opening.

Then I lifted my eyes and saw, and behold, two women coming forward! The wind was in their wings. They had wings like the wings of a stork, and they lifted up the basket between earth and heaven. Then I said to the angel who talked with me, "Where are they taking the basket?" He said to me, "To the land of Shinar, to build a house for it. And when this is prepared, they will set the basket down there on its base."

Poetry, Image, and Symbol

As used in this guide, the three terms in the title of this chapter are considered to be literary modes—not genres but forms that can appear in many genres. They are the material out of which other genres are composed, just as wood is the substance out of which a table is made. Poetry and symbolism are the substance out of which prophecy and apocalypse are composed.

Poetry and Image

Poetry is a form of discourse consisting of imagery and figurative language. A poetic image is any word that names a concrete thing or action. The following excerpt from an oracle of judgment consists of images:

> Foreigners, the most ruthless of nations [Egypt], have cut it down and left it. On the mountains and in all the valleys its branches have fallen, and its boughs have been broken in all the ravines of the land, and all the peoples of the earth have gone away from its shadow and left it. On its fallen trunk dwell all the birds of the heavens, and on its branches are all the beasts of the field. (Ezek. 31:12–13)

In recent years, brain research has demonstrated how the two hemispheres of the human brain process information in contrasting ways. The "left brain" is activated by abstract concepts, logical reasoning, and propositional thinking. The "right brain" deals with sensations, words that name concrete images, and figurative language. Poetry is right-brain discourse, starting with images.

We know from our own experience that we assimilate truth in differing ways. Reading the epistle of Romans gives us the truth about sin and salvation abstractly and theologically. Listening to Handel's oratorio *The Messiah* presents the truth about sin and salvation in a complementary and very different way. Reading statistics about the environmental crisis is far different from reading the surrealistic visions of natural cataclysm in the book of Revelation.

What is the relevance of this to the prophetic and apocalyptic books of the Bible? There is relatively little abstract propositional writing in those parts of the Bible. Nearly everything is embodied in imagery and figurative language. Being able and willing to deal with poetry is a prerequisite to reading and interpreting biblical prophecy and apocalypse.

Poetry is normally embodied in a verse form. In the Bible, this verse form is parallelism—saying the same thing twice or more in consecutive lines in similar grammatical form but in different words and images. For example: "I the LORD search the heart / and test the mind" (Jer. 17:10). "Search" is parallel to "test," and "heart" is parallel to "mind." Approximately half of the prophetic and apocalyptic content of the Bible is couched in verse form, and the other half in prose. But this contrast is more apparent than real. If a prose passage consists primarily of imagery and figurative language, it is known as prose poetry or poetic prose. The prose of the prophetic and apocalyptic is poetic prose, and all the rules of poetry apply.

It is not my purpose to give a complete introduction to poetry in this guide, but here is a list of the main figures of speech in addition to image and imagery:

- metaphor: an implied comparison between two things that does not use the explicit formula "like" or "as"
- simile: an explicit comparison between two things that uses the formula "like" or "as"
- personification: portraying nonhuman phenomena in human terms (very prevalent in prophetic writing)
- apostrophe: direct address to something absent as though present and capable of responding; by slight extension, an address to something that is present (such as a mountain) but incapable of actually responding
- hyperbole: conscious exaggeration for the sake of effect

If we are simply reading a passage privately, we may choose not to subject the poetry of the prophetic and apocalyptic parts of the Bible to close analysis, but if we are teaching a passage, that is not an option. In any piece of writing, the content (the "what" of the utterance) is embodied in a specific form (the "how"). Without interacting with the poetic form of prophecy and apocalypse, we have no access to the content.

It is possible to relate the poetic medium of the prophetic and apocalyptic parts of the Bible to their visionary qualities. Poets are always playing the game of make-believe, envisioning things that we know are not literally true. They prefer the non-literal to the literal. We can profitably reflect on why the prophets and apocalyptic writers rely heavily on poetry and images.

LEARNING BY DOING

It would be easy for me to bypass an exercise on what is obvious, namely, that the prophetic and apocalyptic parts of the Bible rely on poetry. But it is important that we let the reality of that sink in. The following passage will enable you to identify the specific features of poetry that appear, and draw out the meanings embodied in each one:

> Behold, the LORD has one who is mighty and strong;
>   like a storm of hail, a destroying tempest,
> like a storm of mighty, overflowing waters,
>   he casts down to the earth with his hand.
> The proud crown of the drunkards of Ephraim
>   will be trodden underfoot;
> and the fading flower of its glorious beauty,
>   which is on the head of the rich valley,
> will be like a first-ripe fig before the summer:
>   when someone sees it, he swallows it
>   as soon as it is in his hand.
>
> In that day the LORD of hosts will be a crown of glory,
>   and a diadem of beauty, to the remnant of his people,
> and a spirit of justice to him who sits in judgment,
>   and strength to those who turn back the battle at the
>   gate. (Isa. 28:2–6)

Symbolism

It may be risky to elevate one technique, or mode, above others in regard to the multifaceted genres of prophecy and apocalypse, but if we think in terms of what actually embodies the meanings, we can at least say that no technique is more important than symbolism. Even the poetic passages just considered often involve symbolism. A preliminary observation is that although there are many symbols in the prophets, symbolism is even more pervasive in apocalyptic writing.

A symbol is an image, character, setting, or event that exists in its own right (even if it is fantastic rather than real), but also points to or represents one or more other things. The following verse is an example of symbolism on a simple level:

Break forth together into singing,
    you waste places of Jerusalem,
for the LORD has comforted his people;
    he has redeemed Jerusalem. (Isa. 52:9)

A commonsense rule of thumb for determining that an image needs to be interpreted symbolically is that it does not make complete or adequate sense at a purely literal level. Literally, Jerusalem is a physical city. A physical place cannot be redeemed in the spiritual sense that this verse asserts. So what does the city of Jerusalem symbolize? As is often the case, symbolic meanings depend not only on the context in which a symbol appears, but also (or even primarily) on traditional meanings in a culture or body of literature. Jerusalem was the capital city of the nation of Israel and therefore a symbol of the nation. Even more, it was the site of the temple and the center of worship for the nation. But the symbolism in this passage and elsewhere is even more extensive than the Old Testament people of Israel. In this oracle of salvation, Jerusalem symbolizes the total body of believers in all places and times. These are the "Jerusalem" that is redeemed.

If we turn to the book of Revelation (the Bible's chief example of apocalypse), we can see that symbolism is at the heart of the enterprise. Here is an example:

> The first angel blew his trumpet, and there followed hail
> and fire, mixed with blood, and these were thrown upon
> the earth. And a third of the earth was burned up, and a
> third of the trees were burned up, and all green grass was
> burned up. (8:7)

This is a picture of natural cataclysm, but when and where and why? The passage symbolizes God's judgment against an evil world, in the specific form of the physical destruction of the earth. That does not exhaust what we can see in the passage, but the point is that this is not a literal picture, as if exactly one-third of the earth will be burned up. These graphic details symbolize God's judgment and punishment of the evil earthly order.

Symbolic Reality

Prophetic and apocalyptic writers often take symbolism to a higher level: symbolic reality. Realistic literature portrays representational reality in which the details stand for themselves and create a picture of known reality as we find it in our world. It represents, or "imitates," external reality. By contrast, symbolic reality arises when the chief thing that we encounter in a text is a "forest" of symbols. Nearly everything in such a passage is a symbol. The world created is an imagined symbolic reality.

An example from prophetic literature is Daniel's vision of a man whose body parts are made of different minerals:

> You saw, O king, and behold, a great image. This image,
> mighty and of exceeding brightness, stood before you, and
> its appearance was frightening. The head of this image
> was of fine gold, its chest and arms of silver, its middle
> and thighs of bronze, its legs of iron, its feet partly of iron
> and partly of clay. As you looked, a stone was cut out by
> no human hand, and it struck the image on its feet of iron

and clay, and broke them in pieces. Then the iron, the clay, the bronze, the silver, and the gold, all together were broken in pieces, and became like the chaff of the summer threshing floors; and the wind carried them away, so that not a trace of them could be found. But the stone that struck the image became a great mountain and filled the whole earth. (2:31–35)

If we had only the vision itself as data, we would be mystified by its meaning, but in the verses immediately following (2:36–45) every detail is given a symbolic meaning. The various body parts with their individual minerals, as well as the rock that smashes them, are all symbols of empires or kingdoms. In a passage like this, when every detail is a symbol, the imagined world is one of symbolic reality.

While prophecy *sometimes* presents symbolic reality, apocalypse *regularly* does. The book of Revelation consists almost entirely of symbolic reality. The portrait of Christ in 1:12–16 is an example:

Then I turned to see the voice that was speaking to me, and on turning I saw seven golden lampstands, and in the midst of the lampstands one like a son of man, clothed with a long robe and with a golden sash around his chest. The hairs of his head were white, like white wool, like snow. His eyes were like a flame of fire, his feet were like burnished bronze, refined in a furnace, and his voice was like the roar of many waters. In his right hand he held seven stars, from his mouth came a sharp two-edged sword, and his face was like the sun shining in full strength.

Nearly everything in the passage is a symbol. The seven golden lampstands are the seven churches of chapters 2–3. The son of man standing in the midst of them is Christ. The long robe and golden sash represent Christ as king and priest. The whiteness stands for spiritual purity and splendor. Fire, bronze, and the light of the sun in full strength are an example of enameled imagery, which combines a supernatural brilliance of light and hardness of texture to symbolize the glory and permanence of a transcendent place (heaven) and person (Christ). The seven stars are the angels of the seven churches. The sword is the word, power, and judgment of Christ.

The technique of symbolic reality possesses its own kind of brilliance and excitement. The Narnia chronicles of C. S. Lewis are based on the technique of symbolic reality. So is Dante's *Divine Comedy*. Symbolic reality is a demanding form, but one of its great virtues is that it presents truth in an unexpected way and provides fresh angles of vision.

LEARNING BY DOING

The following passage (Zechariah 3) is a based on the premise of symbolic reality. Whereas sometimes we need a study Bible or commentary to decipher prophetic and apocalyptic symbols, much of the time our own hunches are all we need. That is true of the following vision. The four agents (the prophet, God, Satan, and Joshua the high priest) are not symbols; they are real beings. But virtually all of the scenic details, objects, and actions symbolize something.

> Then he [a man with a measuring line] showed me Joshua
> the high priest standing before the angel of the LORD,
> and Satan standing at his right hand to accuse him. And
> the LORD said to Satan, "The LORD rebuke you, O Satan!
> The LORD who has chosen Jerusalem rebuke you! Is not

this a brand plucked from the fire?" Now Joshua was standing before the angel, clothed with filthy garments. And the angel said to those who were standing before him, "Remove the filthy garments from him." And to him he said, "Behold, I have taken your iniquity away from you, and I will clothe you with pure vestments." And I said, "Let them put a clean turban on his head." So they put a clean turban on his head and clothed him with garments. And the angel of the LORD was standing by.

And the angel of the LORD solemnly assured Joshua, "Thus says the LORD of hosts: If you will walk in my ways and keep my charge, then you shall rule my house and have charge of my courts, and I will give you the right of access among those who are standing here. Hear now, O Joshua the high priest, you and your friends who sit before you, for they are men who are a sign: behold, I will bring my servant the Branch. For behold, on the stone that I have set before Joshua, on a single stone with seven eyes, I will engrave its inscription, declares the LORD of hosts, and I will remove the iniquity of this land in a single day. In that day, declares the LORD of hosts, every one of you will invite his neighbor to come under his vine and under his fig tree."

Apocalypse

pocalyptic literature is one of the "fireworks" genres of the
Bible. There is never a dull moment in apocalyptic writing. The prerequisite to enjoying the apocalyptic passages
in the Bible is letting go of our realistic inclinations and setting
our imaginations free to soar. Interpreting apocalyptic literature is
difficult, but we should not start at the level of interpretation. We
should first abandon ourselves to the imaginative energy and brilliance of what the author has composed. There will be a time for
interpretation later. We first need to go along for the ride.

This chapter ends with a consideration of how to interpret the
details in apocalyptic visions. However, our *first* task is always to
relive the text as fully as possible. The early parts of this chapter
are designed to help chart a path through an apocalyptic text.

Previously Discussed Modes

The two preceding chapters have covered literary modes that
apply to apocalyptic writing. We need to review those modes
before turning to features that are distinctive of apocalyptic literature and not the common property of prophecy and apocalypse.

Apocalyptic literature belongs to the even broader category of visionary writing. Visionary literature creates an alternate world, drastically different from the world in which we live. Settings, agents, and events are otherworldly, with the result that we are aware of having entered a strange world where ordinary rules do not apply. Sometimes the element of strangeness is temporal, as the writer's contemporary situation is projected into an envisioned future where the situation is totally reversed. Alternately, the element of strangeness might be part of the fantasy aspect of apocalypse, as when a goat horn reaches to heaven and knocks some stars down (Dan. 8:9–10).

The following brief apocalyptic vision illustrates the visionary nature of apocalyptic writing:

> And I looked, and behold, a pale [yellowish–green] horse!
> And its rider's name was Death, and Hades followed him.
> And they were given authority over a fourth of the earth,
> to kill with sword and with famine and with pestilence
> and by wild beasts of the earth. (Rev. 6:8)

In addition to possessing visionary qualities, apocalyptic literature is built out of poetry, image, and symbol. A commentary on the book of Revelation is aptly named *A Rebirth of Images*.[3] All of the usual rules for reading and interpreting poetry (including imagery and symbolism) covered in the preceding chapter apply to apocalyptic literature. Isaiah 66:12–14 illustrates the poetic texture that makes up the bulk of apocalyptic visions:

For thus says the LORD:

> "Behold, I will extend peace to her like a river,
>   and the glory of the nations like an overflowing stream;

---

3   Austin Farrer, *A Rebirth of Images: The Making of St. John's Apocalypse* (Eugene, OR: Wipf & Stock, 2007).

and you shall nurse, you shall be carried upon her hip,
   and bounced upon her knees.
As one whom his mother comforts,
   so I will comfort you;
   you shall be comforted in Jerusalem.
You shall see, and your heart shall rejoice;
   your bones shall flourish like the grass;
and the hand of the LORD shall be known to his servants,
   and he shall show his indignation against his enemies."

Nearly every line possesses figurative language or imagery and is thereby poetic.

With the foregoing review of visionary and poetic modes before us, we can turn to further defining features of apocalyptic literature.

Defining Apocalypse

The word "apocalypse" is based on a Greek word meaning "revelation" or "unveiling." What is unveiled in apocalyptic literature? Primarily events that will happen at the end of history. The word "apocalyptic" is synonymous with the word "eschatological," based on the word "eschaton," which a dictionary defines as "end of the world, end of time, climax of history."

Two qualifications need to be noted. First, in keeping with the open-ended nature of symbolism, some apocalyptic passages can also refer to events surrounding the Old Testament captivities of Israel and Judah, and to the messianic era surrounding the incarnation of Jesus and the salvation that he brought. This relates to prophetic time, which is often multiple. When John says in Revelation 1:1 that he will write about "the things that must soon take place," we need to remember that what was future for John might be past or present for us.

Additionally, some of the things portrayed in apocalyptic literature are eternal realities, or things in our world that are always true. For example, Daniel's vision of God as "the Ancient of days" (Dan. 7:9) is not only a picture of God as he will be at the end of history but as he always exists. The great spiritual battle between good and evil that organizes apocalyptic reality has been raging since the fall. The biblical concept of "the last days" is very elastic. Paul's statement to Timothy of what people will be like "in the last days" (2 Tim. 3:1–9) is a picture of what has been going on starting in the first century AD and earlier. Nonetheless, even when we read apocalyptic visions of what is perennially happening, we have the feeling that these things will be *ultimately* true at the end of history. The formula "even more so" hovers over apocalyptic literature.

Cosmic Battle

If we take a wide-angle view of what happens in apocalyptic literature, we see a great cosmic conflict between good and evil. On opposing sides we find God and Satan, the saints of God and the followers of Satan. Descriptions of apocalyptic writing regularly use the word "dualism" as a defining trait. This is a view of the universe as divided between forces of good and evil—not in the sense that God is equal with Satan, but in tribute to the great spiritual divide that lies at the heart of the universe. Jesus' picture of the final division of sheep and goats at the last judgment epitomizes the dualism of apocalyptic literature (Matt. 25:31–46).

Apocalypse is a battle story, and this element of conflict provides a helpful overarching framework within which to fit the details in the text. A given passage might present one combatant, or side, rather than a conflict between the two sides, but we assimilate even such passages as part of a story of conflict. Here is a typical apocalyptic vision based on the battle motif: "Then the LORD will go out and fight against those nations as when he fights on a day of battle" (Zech. 14:3). Or this: "And I saw a beast rising out of the sea, with ten horns and seven heads . . . It was allowed to make war on the saints and to conquer them" (Rev. 13:1, 7). A great battle between good and evil is obviously going on in apocalyptic literature.

In keeping with the cosmic scope of the battle, the agents are rarely ordinary people. Reality in apocalyptic visions is elevated above ordinary standards. The agents in apocalyptic visions are often such visionary beings as a mysterious "beast rising out of the earth" (Rev. 13:11), or "the king of the south" who attacks "the king of the north" (Dan. 11:40), or horses that are dispatched to "patrol the earth" (Zech. 6:7). One of the most helpful ways to navigate any work of literature is to compare it in our minds to other similar literary works. If the picture of a great "king of the north" who "throw[s] up siegeworks and take[s] a well-fortified city" (Dan. 11:15) reminds us of *Beowulf* or *The Lord of the Rings*, that is a great advantage as we navigate an apocalyptic text. We should not suppress our awareness of parallels in extra-biblical literature; they can be a great asset.

The magnification of the proportions of battle in apocalyptic literature makes it more than ordinary conflict. This is in keeping with the "end-times" nature of the events. We should think in terms of "a battle to end all battles" as we read apocalyptic visions in the Bible. At this point the cosmic scope of apocalypse plays a role. Often the setting is not a localized place on earth but the whole earth, including sea and sky. The battle might be in the heavens rather than on earth. The combatants are usually whole nations or large armies.

An important aspect of apocalyptic literature is the final triumph of good and defeat of evil. The battle is not a battle between equals, but this does not minimize the strength of the life-or-death struggle. The power of evil in apocalyptic literature is terrifying and often drives us to temporary despair as we read and contemplate. At a given moment the customary motif of battlefield *suspense* enters our minds. But there is no ultimate suspense about the outcome, and it does not hurt the effect at all if we take a sneak peek at the ending of the story. Apocalypse is a genre of the happy ending. The book of Revelation ends with a hero on a white horse who kills a dragon, marries his bride, celebrates the wedding with a feast, and lives happily ever after in a palace glittering with jewels.

One more dimension of apocalyptic conflict needs to be noted. The conflict is not simply a battle between good and evil, but also a contrast between this age and the age to come. This is not provable from a single passage but from the overall movement in the book of Revelation. On the "present evil age" side, we find visions of chaos and collapse—a horror story. These disasters are understood to be happening in ordinary history. After repeated cycles of increasingly dire catastrophes and warnings, a final judgment destroys evil conclusively.

On the other side are repeated pictures of eternal reward and glorification in heaven, conceived as occurring not in history but after it. In prophetic writing, visions of blessing are mainly part of a back-and-forth rhythm between judgment and restoration, conceived as part of life in history. By contrast, glory and blessing in apocalypse are final and eternal, occurring in the age to come.

To summarize, there is a heightened contrast in apocalyptic literature between misery and destruction during history in its final phases, and heavenly reward conceived as something beyond history. We might picture a foreground scene of chaos and motion, and over it a solid mass of light.

Special Categories of Symbolism

In addition to symbolism and symbolic reality in general (as previously covered), apocalyptic visions make use of special categories of symbols. While these can appear anywhere in literature, they occur in concentrated fashion in apocalyptic visions. One category is animals that appear not only as part of the strange world motif but that also possess symbolic meanings. Christ is symbolized by a lamb (Rev. 5:6), and Satan appears as a dragon (Rev. 12:9). In the visions of Daniel 8:1–8, a ram and a goat symbolize political power and perhaps specific empires or the forces of evil in a generalized apocalyptic sense.

Color symbolism is a second category. As with animal characters, some colors that appear in apocalyptic writing are simply part of the visionary quality, while at other times the colors have symbolic meaning. The white garments of the saints (Rev. 3:18; 19:14) symbolize spiritual purity. A red horse (Rev. 6:4) symbolizes slaughter in warfare and a black horse (Rev. 6:5) death. The purple and scarlet cloth of the world empire "Babylon" (actually Rome) in Revelation 18:12 represents affluence and mercantile prosperity.

We also find number symbols. They are bewildering to modern readers but may have been a kind of code language in Bible times. The numbers 3, 7, 10, and 12 are good numbers that symbolize completeness, perfection, or victory. The number 6 is a sinister number similar to our bad-luck 13, approaching the perfection of 7 but falling short. Three and a half years (1,260 days) signal a short time, often in contexts of the temporary reign of evil. The number of the redeemed—144,000—symbolizes completeness (four-square symbolism of 12 times 12, and all 12 tribes represented) and magnitude (inasmuch as 1,000 symbolized a multitude in ancient times). The entire book of Revelation is based on patterns of 7 (letters to 7 churches, 7 seals, 7 trumpets, etc.); it is a fair inference that the number 7 symbolizes completeness.

It is impossible to explore all categories of apocalyptic symbolism. The following selective list is one that you can detect on your own: garments, trumpets, thunder and lightning, high and low, light and darkness, temple, drunkenness, winepress, fire, and harvest. I list these to prompt my readers to think in terms of clusters of images that become familiar as we read more and more apocalyptic literature.

"This Present Evil Age": The Theme of Destruction

With this unit and the following, we move from matters of strictly literary form to ones of theme and content, but they are essential to an understanding of apocalyptic discourse. Together the themes of destruction and renewal constitute a juxtaposition and rhythm possessing some of the quality of a plot conflict.

Apocalyptic literature has no corner on the denunciation of evil in society. Prophecy is equally (or more) focused on the exposure of human vice and the corruptness of institutions. But in prophecy the denunciation of evil is woven into a tapestry of calls to repent and promises of God's mercy and restoration. Despite the extravagance of the imagery of judgment and God's anger against sinful humanity, in prophetic literature we never get the impression that God has reached a point of no return. In fact, nearly all prophetic books swing back and forth between predictions of judgment and promises of God's favor. Sometimes the prophet jumps from one to the other without transition, as in this passage:

> All the sinners of my people shall die by the sword,
>   who say, "Disaster shall not overtake or meet us."
> In that day I will raise up
>   the booth of David that is fallen
> and repair its breaches,
>   and raise up its ruins
> and rebuild it as in the days of old. (Amos 9:10–11)

By contrast, in apocalypse the time for repentance is past. God's judgment is portrayed as moving in a crescendo toward final destruction. In the book of Revelation, scenes of cosmic collapse and natural cataclysm unfold in cycles moving toward a final conflagration and casting of evildoers into hell. There are no scenes of repentance and restoration but the opposite: people "did not repent of the works of their hands nor give up worshiping demons and idols of gold and silver and bronze and stone and wood" (9:20). Instead of the faithful being exhorted to repent, they are repeatedly admonished to endure to the end, as encapsulated in passages such as the following:

- "The one who endures to the end will be saved" (Matt. 24:13).
- "Hold fast what you have, so that no one may seize your crown" (Rev. 3:11).
- "Here is a call for the endurance of the saints" (Rev. 14:12).

LEARNING BY DOING

Revelation 8:6–9 is brief but sufficient for you to apply what was said about the motif of apocalyptic destruction:

> Now the seven angels who had the seven trumpets prepared to blow them.
>
> The first angel blew his trumpet, and there followed hail and fire, mixed with blood, and these were thrown upon the earth. And a third of the earth was burned up, and a third of the trees were burned up, and all green grass was burned up.

> The second angel blew his trumpet, and something like
> a great mountain, burning with fire, was thrown into the
> sea, and a third of the sea became blood. A third of the
> living creatures in the sea died, and a third of the ships
> were destroyed.

"Behold, I Am Making All Things New": The Theme of Renewal

Because prophecy and apocalypse both feature bad-news and good-news passages, it is easy to be misled into thinking that they are identical. The preceding module showed that judgment in prophecy is temporary and conditional, that repentance is what God seeks and often finds in his covenant people, and that judgment nearly always shifts to mercy and restoration. In apocalypse, however, judgment is final.

Something similar happens with the good-news passages in the two genres. In prophecy, the oracles of salvation portray a restoration of what had been lost through human sinfulness and its punishment, as seen in the following two examples:

- "For behold, days are coming, declares the LORD, when I will restore the fortunes of my people, Israel and Judah, . . . and I will bring them back to the land that I gave to their fathers" (Jer. 30:3).
- "Thus says the LORD: Behold, I will restore the fortunes of the tents of Jacob" (Jer. 30:18).

By contrast, the premise of apocalyptic is total destruction followed by new creation. The motif of new heavens and a new earth is the most famous formulation of this theme, as in Isaiah 65:17:

For behold, I create new heavens
    and a new earth,
and the former things shall not be remembered
    or come into mind.

This is not a vision of transformation but of creation and new beginnings. An implied point of apocalypse is that human society and the earthly order are too far gone to be salvageable; only total destruction and replacement by something new is possible.

LEARNING BY DOING

The foregoing module is brief, but on the basis of it, what would you say about the following passage if you were teaching it to a group?

> Then I saw a new heaven and a new earth, for the first heaven and the first earth had passed away, and the sea was no more. And I saw the holy city, new Jerusalem, coming down out of heaven from God, prepared as a bride adorned for her husband. And I heard a loud voice from the throne saying, "Behold, the dwelling place of God is with man. He will dwell with them, and they will be his people, and God himself will be with them as their God. He will wipe away every tear from their eyes, and death shall be no more, neither shall there be mourning, nor crying, nor pain anymore, for the former things have passed away."
>
> And he who was seated on the throne said, "Behold, I am making all things new." Also he said, "Write this down, for these words are trustworthy and true." And he said to me,

"It is done! I am the Alpha and the Omega, the beginning and the end. To the thirsty I will give from the spring of the water of life without payment. The one who conquers will have this heritage, and I will be his God and he will be my son. But as for the cowardly, the faithless, the detestable, as for murderers, the sexually immoral, sorcerers, idolaters, and all liars, their portion will be in the lake that burns with fire and sulfur, which is the second death." (Rev. 21:1–8)

Addendum

The material covered in this chapter up to this point has made a clear distinction between prophetic and apocalyptic literature. I do not wish to modify that line of division, but what might have been lost in the discussion is that the prophetic books contain apocalyptic passages.

How do we know when ordinary prophecy has morphed into an apocalyptic vision? The criterion is whether we believe that the prophet is describing something that will happen at the end of human history or in the age to come. Sometimes this might be an added level of meaning to a passage that can also be interpreted as describing events that fall within historical time. Whenever a passage seems to us to be speaking of the end-times, it has become apocalyptic (perhaps along with other levels of meaning).

There are many such passages in the prophetic books. Here is an example from Isaiah 60:18–21:

Violence shall no more be heard in your land,
    devastation or destruction within your borders;
you shall call your walls Salvation,
    and your gates Praise.

The sun shall be no more
  your light by day,
nor for brightness shall the moon
  give you light;
but the LORD will be your everlasting light,
  and your God will be your glory.
Your sun shall no more go down,
  nor your moon withdraw itself;
for the LORD will be your everlasting light,
  and your days of mourning shall be ended.
Your people shall all be righteous;
  they shall possess the land forever,
the branch of my planting, the work of my hands,
  that I might be glorified.

These realities will not be realized in ordinary history, and by virtue of that the passage places itself into the category of apocalyptic writing.

Interpreting Apocalyptic Symbols

We come finally to the question of interpretation. To what do the symbols refer? The fact that apocalypse presents its content indirectly in the form of symbols does not mean that it does not present truth and reality. It only means that the realities are portrayed symbolically rather than literally. What is the referent of a warrior on a black horse carrying a pair of scales and announcing the cost of food (Rev. 6:5–6)? What does Daniel have in mind with his picture of those who lie in the earth awaking and shining like the stars forever and ever (Dan. 12:2–3)?

The tendency of "prophecy lovers" and biblical scholars is to turn apocalyptic writings into a set of esoterica (something rare and mysterious and known only to a few). I propose instead that we go for obvious interpretations and regard the details as refer-ring to familiar biblical images of the end. The following list is a summary of what the Bible and Christian belief based on it believe will characterize the end-times:

- moral and spiritual degeneration in human society (including "the lawless one" as described in 2 Thess. 2:8–12)
- a spirit of apostasy (including Antichrist and others who mislead people)
- cataclysmic natural and military disasters
- great tribulation and persecution for believers
- the *parousia* ("arrival"), or second coming of Christ
- the millennium (however interpreted)
- intermediate and final judgment (including banishment of unrepentant evildoers to hell)
- final dissolution of earthly reality
- glorification of believers in new heavens and new earth

Most of what we find in the apocalyptic visions of the Bible can be readily related to these end-times realities.

A helpful text to which we can relate the details of the book of Revelation is the Olivet Discourse of Jesus (Matthew 24–25), supplemented by scattered additional apocalyptic passages spo-ken by Jesus. An example of the latter is Luke 23:29–30: "For behold, the days are coming . . . when they will begin to say to the mountains, 'Fall on us,' and to the hills, 'Cover us.'" This is the same event to which Revelation 6:16 refers: "calling to the mountains and rocks, 'Fall on us and hide us from the face of him who is seated on the throne.'"

Jesus' Olivet Discourse outlines a sequence of end-times events to which we can repeatedly relate passages in the book of Revelation:

- false teachers, war, famine, and earthquakes (24:3–8)
- a time of tribulation for believers (24:9–22)
- false teachers, working signs (24:23–28)
- natural disasters and Christ's coming to gather the elect (24:29–31)
- final judgment (a series of parables in 25:1–30, plus expository teaching about the final judgment in vv. 31–46)

How does this work itself out? The four-horse visions of Revelation 6:1–8 present a symbolic narrative of war, famine, and death corresponding to Jesus' account of what will happen early in the end-times (Matt. 24:3–8).

I do not mean to minimize the "far out" nature of the details that appear in the text, such as this: "the sun became black as sackcloth, the full moon became like blood, and the stars of the sky fell to the earth" (Rev. 6:12–13). But the list of familiar images of the end gives us confidence as we navigate the text. The just-quoted passage is a picture of the cataclysmic destruction of nature that will happen (an item on my list of images of the end).

At the risk of overloading my readers, I share an even simpler and broader list than the two that appear above. In my introductory remarks when teaching long works of literature, I use the formula "images of . . ." as an organizing framework for the work I am about to teach. The following is my list of images for apocalyptic literature:

- battle
- evil
- good
- heaven or glory
- mystery
- judgment
- redemption

- worship
- cataclysm (sudden and violent destruction of nature)

We can make adequate sense and be edified by many apocalyptic passages by relating them to simple, obvious categories like these.

Knowing that a lot of nonsense has been perpetuated by relating apocalyptic details to specific historical events, I broach the following suggestion with a bit of reluctance. Because the symbols and images of apocalyptic writing are open-ended, I do not find it objectionable to read these passages with an eye on a weekly news magazine and the daily newspaper and television news. With the arrival of the ecological crisis, I assimilate the visions of the cataclysmic destruction of natural forces in the book of Revelation far differently than I did half a century ago. I do not see how we can fail to see the daily news of terrorism and nations threatening each other in the visions of Revelation and Daniel.

LEARNING BY DOING

The following passage from Revelation gives you ample scope to try your hand at interpreting apocalyptic symbols and visions:

> Then I saw another beast rising out of the earth. It had two horns like a lamb and it spoke like a dragon. It exercises all the authority of the first beast in its presence, and makes the earth and its inhabitants worship the first beast, whose mortal wound was healed. It performs great signs, even making fire come down from heaven to earth in front of people, and by the signs that it is allowed to work in the presence of the beast it deceives those who dwell on earth, telling them to make an image for the

beast that was wounded by the sword and yet lived. And it was allowed to give breath to the image of the beast, so that the image of the beast might even speak and might cause those who would not worship the image of the beast to be slain. Also it causes all, both small and great, both rich and poor, both free and slave, to be marked on the right hand or the forehead, so that no one can buy or sell unless he has the mark, that is, the name of the beast or the number of its name . . .

Then I looked, and behold, on Mount Zion stood the Lamb, and with him 144,000 who had his name and his Father's name written on their foreheads. And I heard a voice from heaven like the roar of many waters and like the sound of loud thunder. The voice I heard was like the sound of harpists playing on their harps, and they were singing a new song before the throne and before the four living creatures and before the elders. No one could learn that song except the 144,000 who had been redeemed from the earth. It is these who have not defiled themselves with women, for they are virgins. It is these who follow the Lamb wherever he goes. These have been redeemed from mankind as firstfruits for God and the Lamb, and in their mouth no lie was found, for they are blameless. (13:11–17; 14:1–5)

A Miscellany of Prophetic and Apocalyptic Forms

A s unlikely as it may seem, there are still more literary forms and genres shared by prophecy and apocalypse that have not yet been explored in this guide. Are they sufficiently important that leaving them out would be a significant omission? I believe they are. If we combine all of the passages that fall into the categories covered in this chapter, they constitute a major body of material. Reading and teaching these passages under the format of genres discussed up to this point would be deficient.

I have used the label "miscellany" as an umbrella for this chapter. A dictionary defines a miscellany as "a collection of different items; a mixture; an assortment of different pieces of writing." That is an accurate description of what this chapter explores.

Visions of a Coming Golden Age

I need to begin with a reminder that apocalyptic passages can occur in the prophetic books. The reverse of that is also true. For example, the letters to the seven churches in the book of Revelation belong more to the genre of prophecy than apocalypse.

Some of the most resplendent passages in the Bible are what I label "golden age prophecies." They use idealized imagery to evoke a place, society, and life of perfection. The imagery is stylized and stereotyped. Isaiah 11:6–9 is a typical golden age prophecy:

> The wolf shall dwell with the lamb,
>   and the leopard shall lie down with the young goat,
> and the calf and the lion and the fattened calf together;
>   and a little child shall lead them.
> The cow and the bear shall graze;
>   their young shall lie down together;
>   and the lion shall eat straw like the ox.
> The nursing child shall play over the hole of the cobra,
>   and the weaned child shall put his hand on the adder's den.
> They shall not hurt or destroy
>   in all my holy mountain;
> for the earth shall be full of the knowledge of the LORD
>   as the waters cover the sea.

This is one version of a golden age: the peaceable kingdom in a pastoral (rural) mode. The effect is gained through the techniques of reversal and negation, as conditions of violence and strife in our fallen world are simply gone.

Pastoral versions of the golden age are complemented by utopian scenes of civilization and city living. Zechariah 8:3–5 is a famous example:

> Thus says the LORD: I have returned to Zion and will dwell in the midst of Jerusalem, and Jerusalem shall be called the faithful city, and the mountain of the LORD of hosts, the holy mountain. Thus says the LORD of hosts: Old men and old women shall again sit in the streets of Jerusalem, each with staff in hand because of great age.

And the streets of the city shall be full of boys and girls playing in its streets.

With that brief glimpse before us, we can readily recall many prophetic passages that portray city building projects as part of a coming golden age.

It is not my purpose to provide a full analysis of motifs that appear in the golden age prophecies of the Bible or a taxonomy of types of golden age. What I wish to establish is that this is a major genre in the prophetic books, and we need to identify a golden age prophecy when we encounter it. We also need to be receptive of the exhilaration and longing that breathe through such visions.

What is the referent of such pictures of perfection? When will they happen? Situations in literature where multiple levels of meaning are possible at the same time go by the literary term "ambiguity." I believe that the visions of a coming golden age are a preeminent example of ambiguity in the Bible. If we read in an awareness that a remnant of people returned from Babylon to the Promised Land after the captivity, our first impulse is to read the golden age visions as an idealized account of that return. But then as we are reading along we often encounter details that are beyond mere idealization and hyperbole. They are pictures of the age to come (either the millennium or eternity in heaven). But some of these golden age prophecies are quoted in the New Testament as messianic in nature, so we need to add that layer as well.

Doom Song

Exactly opposite to a golden age prophecy is a doom song. We might say that all of the oracles of judgment and apocalyptic visions of destruction are permeated by a sense of doom, but the genre that scholars have labeled "doom song" is more specific than a general sense of doom. A doom song takes as its subject the fall of an evil nation. The downfall is portrayed in vivid detail and can have the flavor of either a taunt or a lament. Before I explore the form in detail, it will be useful to have an example before us. The following passage is an excerpt from an oracle against Tyre (Ezek. 28:6–9):

> Therefore thus says the Lord GOD:
> Because you make your heart
>   like the heart of a god,
> therefore, behold, I will bring foreigners upon you,
>   the most ruthless of the nations;
> and they shall draw their swords against the beauty of
> your wisdom
>   and defile your splendor.
> They shall thrust you down into the pit,
>   and you shall die the death of the slain
>   in the heart of the seas.
> Will you still say, "I am a god,"
>   in the presence of those who kill you,
> though you are but a man, and no god,
>   in the hands of those who slay you?

An initial response might be that this is not distinctively different from the usual oracle of judgment. This is not inaccurate, so the point is partly that the doom song exists in a loose sense quite broadly in the prophetic books. Nonetheless, as I add to my description of the genre, it will become clear why scholars label the oracles against Tyre in Ezekiel 26–28 "doom songs," while being less inclined to call surrounding oracles of judgment by that name.

A common motif in doom songs is the inventory of what will be "no more"—a litany of losses that by their very naming evokes a picture of a prosperity that once was. The following doom song appears in the apocalyptic passage in Revelation 18:21–23, depicting the destruction of a composite or personified Babylon:

Then a mighty angel took up a stone like a great millstone
and threw it into the sea, saying,
"So will Babylon the great city be thrown down with violence,
    and will be found no more;
and the sound of harpists and musicians, of flute players
and trumpeters,
    will be heard in you no more,
and a craftsman of any craft
    will be found in you no more,
and the sound of the mill
    will be heard in you no more,
and the light of a lamp
    will shine in you no more,
and the voice of bridegroom and bride
    will be heard in you no more,
for your merchants were the great ones of the earth,
    and all nations were deceived by your sorcery."

This doom song belongs to a category that has an element of lament—not in the sense of sorrow that the doomed nation has been punished, but in an awareness that it is sad that the situation ended this way when an alternative existed (obeying God and his rules for living). The adjective "elegiac" is sometimes used for doom songs, based on the genre of elegy, or funeral poem.

Before analyzing the genre further, I want to place another example before us to maintain our awareness of the distinctiveness of the form. Isaiah 24:8–11 is part of an oracle against the whole earth:

The mirth of the tambourines is stilled,
    the noise of the jubilant has ceased,
    the mirth of the lyre is stilled.

No more do they drink wine with singing;
    strong drink is bitter to those who drink it.
The wasted city is broken down;
    every house is shut up so that none can enter.
There is an outcry in the streets for lack of wine;
    all joy has grown dark;
    the gladness of the earth is banished.

An oracle of judgment does not need to state a litany of losses before we call it a "doom song," and it is not inappropriate to use that label with oracles of judgment more generally. Nonetheless, it is essential that we at least use the designation "doom song" for passages that use the motif of things that are absent.

In an added bit of complexity, even though doom songs usually predict a coming judgment against an evil nation, they are often phrased in the present tense. The effect is that the judgment is so certain that it is as if the destruction has already occurred.

As noted earlier, some doom songs evoke a sense of lament and sadness over the lost potential of an evil nation. But sometimes the song is a taunt. Isaiah 14:3–4 is a lead-in to a doom song against Babylon, and it makes the taunting intention explicit:

When the LORD has given you rest from your pain and turmoil and the hard service with which you were made to serve, you will take up this taunt against the king of Babylon.

This passage uses the future tense, but the doom song that follows is phrased in the present tense. The most famous passage is Isaiah 14:12:

How you are fallen from heaven,
    O Day Star, son of Dawn!

How you are cut down to the ground,
    you who laid the nations low!

The features of the doom song that I have noted are helpful tools of identification. The methods of analysis are the ordinary ones that we use for oracles of judgment and satire (and where relevant the taunt).

Woe Formula

From grand genres like the golden age prophecy and doom song, I narrow the focus to what scholars call a "formula"—a recurrent phrase used in a given situation. The woe formula can appear in either prophecy or apocalypse, and can be uttered by either God or a prophet. Here are five examples:

- "Woe to those who call evil good and good evil" (Isa. 5:20).
- "Woe to him who builds his house by unrighteousness" (Jer. 22:13, uttered against Shallum, king of Judah).
- "Woe to those who are at ease in Zion" (Amos 6:1).
- "Woe to him who builds a town with blood / and founds a city on iniquity" (Hab. 2:12).
- "Woe to you, O earth and sea, for the devil has come down to you in great wrath" (Rev. 12:12).

This list shows two things: (1) the range of subjects on whom woe is pronounced is wide; and (2) the woe formula usually appears in oracles of judgment or passages of satire. It is accurate to think of the rudimentary woe formula as the *vehicle* for an oracle of judgment or a satire.

The woe formula does not require any specific rules of interpretation. It is simply useful to identify it when we read it.

Surrealism

If "surrealism" is in your active vocabulary, you are likely to have encountered the term in connection with modern painting. The aim of the surrealistic movement was to give visual expression to the subconscious, including its dreamlike dimension. The techniques for that enterprise were illogical juxtaposition of bits and pieces of external reality, as well as the creation of strange and unlifelike creatures. The materials with which surrealistic painters created came from real life (eyes, faces, fruit, and virtually anything else), but the depiction of these pieces is dislocated, strange, and shocking.

I explain below why I find it useful to have the category of surrealism in my awareness as I read the prophetic and apocalyptic books of the Bible, but my discussion will make more sense if we have an example before us. Ezekiel 10:12–14 comes from a vision that describes four seraphim who are accompanied by wheels:

> And their whole body, their rims, and their spokes, their wings, and the wheels were full of eyes all around—the wheels that the four of them had. As for the wheels, they were called in my hearing "the whirling wheels." And every one had four faces: the first face was the face of the cherub, and the second face was a human face, and the third the face of a lion, and the fourth the face of an eagle.

I find it easy to visualize what a painter would do with this scene. The basic technique is to take objects from the known world, distort them, put them together in a total picture that could never exist in reality, and by those means get us to focus even more strongly on the individual items such as the four faces.

Ezekiel 10:12–14 comes from a prophetic book, but the techniques of surrealism are even more prevalent in apocalyptic writing. Here is an example from Revelation 13:1–2:

And I saw a beast rising out of the sea, with ten horns and seven heads, with ten diadems on its horns and blasphemous names on its heads. And the beast that I saw was like a leopard; its feet were like a bear's, and its mouth was like a lion's mouth. And to it the dragon gave his power and his throne and great authority.

When I read a passage like this for devotions, I initially despair of making sense of it. One avenue toward coping with that discomfort is to extract the symbolism of the scene. But didn't the author intend that we relish the images first? For me, to think in terms of surrealism makes the passage fall into place at the surface level of imagery.

The following is a list of common surrealistic techniques that we find in the prophetic and apocalyptic books:

- the visible world around us as the starting point from which the author gathers material
- bringing common objects into unrealistic combinations (making the ordinary suddenly seem extraordinary or strange)
- distortion (sometimes called caricature) of the objects themselves, so that the parts, too, and not simply their juxtaposition, seem strange
- intermixture of fantasy elements (e.g., a dragon) to complement realistic objects

Overall, we can say that surrealism combines the familiar and the unfamiliar.

There are no special interpretive tools that surrealism requires beyond what has been already covered in this guide. But at the level of reading, there are advantages to having surrealism on our radar screen. We can somewhat tame the wild side of a surrealistic passage if we understand the techniques listed above. There is "a method to the madness," as the common saying has it. Above all, we need to abandon realistic expectations in deference to the fantastic. Having the right expectations always helps.

Why do prophetic and apocalyptic writers use surrealism? Surrealism has arresting strangeness and grabs our attention. The prophets and apocalyptic visionaries wish to overcome our numbness to truth brought on by sheer familiarity, and also to challenge our assumption that what we see around us is the only reality that exists. Related to that, one effect of surrealism is that it creates a sense of mystery, which is certainly appropriate when a writer portrays supernatural reality.

The Grotesque Imagination

I am a little hesitant to introduce the subject of the grotesque imagination into this guide, but I think it is required in order to give an accurate account of prophetic and apocalyptic literature in the Bible. According to a dictionary definition, something is grotesque if it is repulsive, ugly, or distorted. When I teach Dante's *Inferno*, I tell my students that grotesquery is one of Dante's greatest skills. In view of certain things that have already been covered in this guide, it cannot come as a complete surprise that we find an element of the grotesque in the prophetic and apocalyptic parts of the Bible.

I offer the following passages as examples of what I have in mind:

- "Those who sanctify and purify themselves to go into the gardens, following on in the midst, eating pig's flesh and abomination and mice, shall come to an end together, declares the LORD" (Isa. 66:17).
- "a wild donkey used to the wilderness, / in her heat sniffing the wind" (Jer. 2:24).

- "And I saw the woman, drunk with the blood of the saints" (Rev. 17:6).
- "She lusted after lovers with genitals as large as a donkey's and emissions like those of a horse" (Ezek. 23:20, NLT).
- "The third angel poured out his bowl into the rivers and the springs of water, and they became blood" (Rev. 16:4).
- "Instead of perfume there will be rottenness; /. . . and instead of well-set hair, baldness" (Isa. 3:24).

I do not wish to overstate the incidence of grotesquery in the prophetic and apocalyptic books. It is important to know that this element is present so we can be prepared for it when we read it (doubly and triply so in public settings). For example, the imagery of whoring and whore as metaphors for spiritual faithlessness to God appears some five dozen times in the Old Testament prophets. We can say that grotesquery is an important minor motif.

Horror Story

I am an advocate of the view that when we read literature we often encounter works that have *affinities to* certain literary genres without being full-fledged examples. I believe that biblical prophecy and apocalypse regularly evoke terror, and that this strand can be said to be related to the genre of horror story.

A horror story is one in which the evocation of horror and fear is a main ingredient. There are certain categories of horror. Battle stories awaken fear with physical details of bodily mutilation and pain. Apocalyptic visions elicit fear through scenes of national disaster. Monster stories produce their effects through supernatural beings with more-than-natural power.

Biblical prophecy and apocalypse frequently depict horror in their oracles and visions of God's punishment of evil. Below is a sampling:

- "And great hailstones, about one hundred pounds each, fell from heaven on people" (Rev. 16:21).
- "Terror, pit, and snare
     are before you . . .
  He who flees from the terror
     shall fall into the pit,
  and he who climbs out of the pit
     shall be caught in the snare" (Jer. 48:43–44).
- "And the peoples will be as if burned to lime, like thorns cut down, that are burned in the fire." (Isa. 33:12)
- "In appearance the locusts were like horses prepared for battle . . . They have tails and stings like scorpions, and their power to hurt people for five months is in their tails" (Rev. 9:7, 10).

What are we to make of the presence of horror story motifs in the prophetic and apocalyptic parts of the Bible? They are part of the theme of God's judgment against evil and those who practice it without repentance. Perhaps the best commentary on this situation is a statement made by seventeenth-century Anglican preacher Jeremy Taylor, who wrote, "God threatens terrible things if we will not be happy," that is, happy in the person and promises of God, including the promise of eternal life in heaven.

LEARNING BY DOING

This chapter has covered six literary forms: golden age prophecy, doom song, woe formula, surrealism, the grotesque imagination, and horror story. The following list of passages (to be consulted in your own Bible) includes an example of each of these, but the list does not follow the same order as the preceding discussion.

- Isaiah 28:8
- Isaiah 13:19–22
- Revelation 16:8–13
- Joel 2:23–27
- Ezekiel 1:4–14
- Isaiah 6:4–5

9

Structure and Organization of Prophetic and Apocalyptic Literature

T he brevity of this chapter should not be construed as meaning that it is unimportant. We will not read the prophetic and apocalyptic parts of the Bible with relish, and we will not gravitate to them naturally, if we cannot negotiate their unique patterns of organization. Unless we understand how prophetic and apocalyptic discourse is structured, these parts of the Bible will remain closed books.

What *Not* to Expect

Before we look at how prophetic and apocalyptic books are organized, we will benefit from clearing the deck of inaccurate conceptions. The two most common formats found in literature generally—narrative structure and logical arrangement—are *not* operative in the prophetic and apocalyptic books of the Bible.

Narrative Structure

Stories are usually structured on the premise of a smooth narrative flow that follows a sequence of beginning-middle-end. Even when a narrative has multiple story lines (the exception rather than the rule), each of these follows a linear sequence of events. These events are causally related, with one producing the next one. Narrative format is continuous. Usually there is a single unifying action, such as David's conquest of Goliath in the David-and-Goliath story.

Prophetic and apocalyptic genres are not structured as a story. There is no smooth and continuous chain of events. There is no unifying action, and there is no plot as that concept is commonly used.

Logical Organization

The other common format with which we operate day by day is the logical organization of an essay. It consists of a main thesis accompanied by subordinate generalizations. We assimilate it as a coherent collection of ideas logically arranged.

No one would place prophetic and apocalyptic genres into this category. They are not essays with subordinate generalizations. In fact, I doubt that *any* passage in the prophetic and apocalyptic books is structured as an essay with subordinate generalizations.

We need to start, then, with an awareness that our two most customary formats for written discourse—narrative and essay—do not account for the prophetic and apocalyptic parts of the Bible.

The Overall Format

We need to begin at the broadest level, with the individual prophetic and apocalyptic books. We immediately need to acknowledge that there are prophetic and apocalyptic segments in books that are not overall prophetic or apocalyptic books. For example, Matthew 23 is a prophetic denunciation by Jesus, and the following two chapters, the Olivet Discourse, are an apocalyptic discourse.

Even though we will eventually see that prophetic and apocalyptic books differ in their organization at a minute level, at a more general level they are the same. The most natural term for prophetic and apocalyptic books is "anthology." An anthology is a collection of self-contained units. The main point of unity is that all of the individual items appear in the same book or collection. There is no continuity or linear sequence that carries through from beginning to end.

The idea of an anthology solves a lot of problems. It spares us from looking for sequential continuity. Freed from that dead end, we can look for an alternative format. A self-contained oracle or apocalyptic vision is just that—self–contained. When we finish it, we have reached closure on that particular unit.

I need to add that an anthology is not a book arranged by chapters. Any book arranged by chapters is based on the premise of continuity and overall unity. Individual chapters are part of an ongoing story or argument. By contrast, the entries in the table of contents of an anthology are titles of freestanding units, complete in themselves.

Several additional terms can fill out the picture. I regularly use the phrase "kaleidoscopic structure" when teaching works that keep shifting without continuity from one unit to the next. The concept of a "mosaic" is equally accurate. Literary scholars use the formula "encyclopedic form" to cover the same phenomenon of a collection of discrete units that lack sequential continuity.

Are there any elements of unity and coherence beyond the unity of an anthology? There are, as follows:

- Certain genres are by far the most numerous category in prophetic and apocalyptic literature, and these impose a kind of unity in our thinking. The genres are oracle in prophecy and vision in apocalypse.

- Most prophetic and apocalyptic books use the cluster principle in certain parts of them. For example, in several prophetic books we encounter a cluster of oracles against the nations and a cluster of oracles of salvation. The book of Revelation contains numerous sevenfold clusters of visions. We immediately need to note that even in these cases there is other interspersed material within the clusters.

- I have said that the prophetic and apocalyptic books do not follow a linear sequence in which one unit produces the next. In place of sequential flow in the narrative or essay sense, prophetic and apocalyptic books are based on the premise of an accumulation of items in which one is added to the next and so forth. There is a strong repetitive element, with similar material being repeated and gradually making up a bigger and bigger accumulation.

- A prophetic book is a static collection of oracles in which one oracle is followed by the next one. In some (but not all) apocalyptic passages, things are more continuous and fast-moving than that. The right term is "pageant of visions," and we should remember that the vision is the most customary genre in apocalyptic writing. The effect is like watching a video sequence. In Revelation 16, for example, we witness a pageant of seven bowls of wrath, one after the other.

The Micro Level

The foregoing discussion has dealt with prophetic and apocalyptic books at a macro level. That allows us to take a bird's-eye view of the books, but it does not help us when dealing with individual units. I am ready to take a more minute look at the individual units. I proceed by putting an actual example before us and then analyzing it.

Isaiah 19:5–8 is typical of what we find in the prophetic books; the passage is part of an oracle of judgment:

> And the waters of the sea will be dried up,
>> and the river will be dry and parched,
> and its canals will become foul,
>> and the branches of Egypt's Nile will diminish and dry up,
>> reeds and rushes will rot away.
> There will be bare places by the Nile,
>> on the brink of the Nile,
> and all that is sown by the Nile will be parched,
>> will be driven away, and will be no more.
> The fishermen will mourn and lament,
>> all who cast a hook in the Nile;
> and they will languish
>> who spread nets on the water.

This is the simplest pattern that we find in the prophetic oracles, namely, a catalog of individual items unified by a single subject. "Catalog" is the customary literary term for a list. In this case, the list consists of individual natural disasters that will engulf Egypt when God instigates his judgment against it. The catalog in which all items are examples of the same thing is the simplest structural form that we find in the prophetic books, and it is the most common form. We can profitably think in terms of theme and variation.

Sometimes, however, the content is more disjointed than the single-topic catalog. The following is an example:

For he said, "Surely they are my people,
   children who will not deal falsely."
   And he became their Savior . . .
But they rebelled
   and grieved his Holy Spirit;
therefore he turned to be their enemy,
   and himself fought against them.
Then he remembered the days of old,
   of Moses and his people. (Isa. 63:8, 10–11a)

As the prophet proclaims this retrospective passage, he swings from remembrance of God's favor, to pondering the covenant people's rebellion and God's judgment against them, to a meditation on God's being gracious to his people. I use the literary concept of "stream of consciousness" for a passage in which the subject keeps shifting. This means that the thought follows the thought process of the speaker, with one thought prompting a related or contrasting one and then another related but different thought.

Another structural possibility is narrative. The prophetic and apocalyptic books had a more frequent narrative element than the foregoing discussion may have implied. Revelation 12:7–9 narrates an epic action in brief compass:

Now war arose in heaven, Michael and his angels fighting against the dragon. And the dragon and his angels fought back, but he was defeated, and there was no longer any place for them in heaven. And the great dragon was thrown down, that ancient serpent, who is called the devil and Satan, the deceiver of the whole world—he was thrown down to the earth, and his angels were thrown down with him.

Or Ezekiel 31:16:

> I made the nations quake at the sound of its fall, when I
> cast it down to Sheol with those who go down to the pit.
> And all the trees of Eden, the choice and best of Lebanon,
> all that drink water, were comforted in the world below.

This passage recounts actions that God performed and therefore constitutes a brief narrative.

Yet another pattern of organization is description, usually of a scene and sometimes of a person. Revelation 7:9–10 is an example:

> After this I looked, and behold, a great multitude that
> no one could number, from every nation, from all tribes
> and peoples and languages, standing before the throne
> and before the Lamb, clothed in white robes, with palm
> branches in their hands, and crying out with a loud voice,
> "Salvation belongs to our God who sits on the throne,
> and to the Lamb!"

This passage paints a picture. The scene is ready for filming and includes costumes and stationing of characters in a scene. One commentator on the book of Revelation uses the formula "scenic data."

Summary

The foregoing outline of structural possibilities is not intended to be exhaustive or prescriptive. But we need *some* categories in our minds as a starting point. The prophetic and apocalyptic parts of the Bible are more than a collection of individual verses.

At the macro level, prophetic and apocalyptic books are anthologies of individual units, chiefly of oracles and visions, with interspersed additional subgenres. We do not find a narrative flow or logical principle of thesis and subordinate generalizations. Instead, we find clusters of similar material, an accumulation of items that keeps growing, and the pageant principle.

At the micro level, common principles of organization in brief units include catalog, narrative, and description.